Bank Lending Products & Securities:
A Conventional & Islamic Banking Approach.

Ibrahim Mohammed Lawal

DEDICATION

This Book is dedicated to my late Dad & Brother, Ibrahim Abdullahi and Abubakar Sadiq for their love, care and encouragement.

Published by IISTE Publishing in the United States

ISBN 978-1-62265-155-9, ISBN-10: 1622651553

ACKNOWLEDGEMENTS

All praises and thanks is due to Allah Almighty, the disposer of affairs, the creator, the grantor, the opener of all doors of success, and the all knower of things, who in his infinite mercy had made of possible for me to reach the end of this book.

My profound gratitude goes to my reviewer Dr. Aliyu Tahir of Bayero University, Kano who despite his numerous engagements took time and pains to go through my manuscript and make constructive criticism and useful corrections in order to make this book a reality.

I am also indebted to the Dean Faculty of Social Sciences, Prof. Dahiru Hassan Balami, my Head of Department, Dr. Musa Muhammad, and Dr. Jibir Talba for their fatherly role in making this work a success and to all other lecturers in the department amongst who are Dr. Mohammed Othman Lawan, Dr. Ibrahim Bello, Dr. Fausat Fumilola Ahmed, Dr. Mohammed Danladi Tukur, Dr. Abdulkadir Niran Adedeji, Dr. Bukar Mustapha, Dr. Baba Jidda Malah, Mallam Ahmed Adama for their suggestions, assistance and guidance in the course of this work.

Special thanks goes to my lovely mum and wife, Ketimu Ibrahim and Amina Jibrin for their support, love, care and encouragement so also to my lovely daughters, Ruqayyah and Umm kulthum Mohammed Abdullahi.

My deep appreciation and gratitude goes to Hajja Mairama Lemos, Alhaji Shuaibu Abubakar, Alhaji Mohammed Kolo, Alhaji Bukar Sanda, Hajja Mairo Babagana, Alhaji Mai Sherriff, Hajja Amma Gangaran, Abdullahi Maina for their financial support and encouragement. I will also remain grateful to my Guardian-Rakiya Abubakar her husband Abubakar Sadiq and daughters, Farida Abubakar and Zainab Abubakar for their family love, care and encouragement.

Special gratitude goes to my Branch Managers, Hajja Amine Sheriff, Hajja Gana Ajayi and operations Manager Talatu Silas Sawa for their motherly care and support in making this work a reality and to my colleagues Yusuf Mohammed Yusuf, Ibrahim Mohammed Nur, Ayoola Ogunbuiji, Yahaya Abdullahi Jaji, Allawan Ahmed Tijjani, Stella Adejoh, Zara Jidda Rufai, Sunday Ocheje, Mohammed Isa, Samaila Kida, Kashim Ali, Usman Ali, Haruna Mohammed, Musa Mohammed, Modu Ibrahim, Abdullahi Abdulwahab, Sunday Jonathan, Victory Onyesi, Yagana Shettima, Hadiza Musa for their immense support and advise during this work.

My personal obligation goes to my course mates Umar Babagana Imam, Abdullahi Mohammed, Joan Munakur, Nur Baba Shettima for their support, encouragement in making this work a success and to Dr. Shuaibu Gidado, Hussaini Garba, Engr. Umar Mata, Ibrahim Ali, Aminu Alih, Mohammed Abdullahi, Maimuna Ali, Yusuf Alhaji Mohammed, Hassan Jimba, Fatima & Maryam Jibrin, Mariam Yunusa, I sincerely appreciate your effort in making this work a reality.

Finally, I would like to use this medium to register my appreciation to the management of Heritage Bank Plc, Ramat Polytechnic and Kashim College of Education for their support, time and information they offered to me during the research work.

PREFACE

Islamic banking is considered as an alternative to the conventional form of banking system as it provides financial services in accordance with the *shariah.* The adoption of this form of Islamic banking is gradually taken the centre stage in the parlance of the financial world. This book tries to explore comprehensively both the Islamic and the conventional banking approach in relation to bank Lending products and securities (Collateral). This book is divided into ten chapters.

Chapter one sets out to give an overview of the conventional banking system where its origin, definition and its various types was discussed. It also introduces the concept of lending as well as highlighted the various cannons that govern lending.

Chapter two discusses the major lending products that are obtained in the conventional banking system such as overdraft, import overdraft, import and export finance facility, foreign currency loan, letter of credit confirmation line, invoice discounting facility, local purchase order, term loan, direct credits, leases, loan syndication, specialized loan. The chapter ends by also highlighting some of the retail loans.

Chapter three proceeded by introducing the concept of security (collateral) its various features in order to ascertain when a security is good or not. The chapter ends by highlighting some of the benefits attached when obtaining security (collateral) when it comes to lending.

In chapter four, the various forms of securities that are acceptable by conventional banks was also discussed. Amongst which are land, debenture, stocks and shares, life insurance, cash deposit, guarantee. Other types of securities were also mentioned such as equipment lease agreement, assignment of debts, factoring, bonds and money market instruments.

The concept of Islamic banking was introduced in chapter six, its origin and its current performance in the various regions of the world was discussed. The chapter ends by discussing further the principles that are guiding the operations of Islamic banking.

Chapter six sets out to examine the various sources of funds that are available for the smooth operation of its activities. Basically the sources that are avaibale internally and externally was mentioned.

Chapter seven dwells deeply on the various lending modes that are obtainable in Islamic banks. Amongst which are *Murabahah, Musharakah, Mudarabah,, Ijarah, Istisna'a, Tawarruq, Bai-salam* etc. Chapter eight focuses on security in an Islamic perspective. Its types in islam and also discussed the position of security in Islamic banking on whether it is acceptable or not.

Chapter nine discusses the various forms of securities that are acceptable by *I*slamic banks which was discussed based on an Islamic approach. Amongst which are land, debenture, stocks and shares, insurance *(takaful*), cash deposit, guarantee, Islamic Bond (*Sukuk*) other types of securities were also mentioned such as *Ijarah* lease agreement, assignment of debts (*Hiwalah*), and factoring, Islamic money market instruments. The book ended by examining the difference and the similarities between Islamic banking and the conventional banking

Ibrahim Mohammed Lawal
Maiduguri, Borno State
March,2018

Contents

Chapter One: Overview of Conventional Banking

1.1 Introduction

Banking operations were practiced by almost all known early civilizations, long before 12th AD[1]. Most economists' maintained that "Banking was Italian by birth". Firstly, because the technical word Bank is derived from the Italian word *Banco* which means a table or a bench in which Italian money changers used to display their monies and records and conduct their transactions. Secondly, because they considered that the first bank worth of the name was those established in Venice, Florence, Genoa and Lucca in Italy. [2]Banking is often considered as a modern device of recent origin, but a glance through the pages of financial history dispels the notion of novelty.

Conventional banking that is been practiced globally is interest based and it can either be in form of universal banking or commercial banking. Though there exist other sub-forms of conventional banking like Merchant banking, Mortgage banking etc. Universal banking is a banking system in which banks provide a wide variety of financial services, including commercial and investment services[3]. Universal banking is common in some European countries, including Switzerland, Netherlands, and Japan where as a commercial banking is a financial institution that provides various financial services, such as accepting deposits and issuing loans[4]. This form of conventional banking is mostly practice in Anglo-Saxon countries such as USA, UK etc.

Consequently, no matter the variant conventional banking that is been practiced in any economies of the world, they are considered as financial intermediaries because they mobilize funds from the surplus units to the deficit units and in undertaking such functions the debtor and creditor relationship is established as spelt out in the popular English case of *Foley Vs Hill (1848)* because when the banks receive money from customers, they become debtors and the depositors become Creditors. A reverse of the debtor and Creditor relationship is established when the bank lends

---

[1] Jaffer. K (2012): Comparative study Between Islamic and Conventional Banks; Case study Islamic bank Tanzania. International University of Africa (IUA), Faculty of economics, adminstration. P.4

[2] Abdel kaderChachi,(2005) origin and development of commercial and Islamic banking operations, Islamic economics research Centre king Abdul Aziz Universityvol.18, Jeddah Saudi, page no22

[3] Universal banking; http://www.investopedia.com/terms/u/universalbanking.asp#ixzz4bFLMad00 13/03/2017,10:45

[4]CommercialBank http://www.investopedia.com/terms/c/commercialbank.asp#ixzz4bFLxH456: 13/03/2017,10:45

out such deposits to its customers. In this case, the banks become creditor while the customer (borrower) also becomes the debtor.

Lending as a core function of banks is a very relevant impetus for income generation and at the same time a crippling agent if not properly managed. Thus, it is seen as a "good servant" and a "bad master" to banks. Bank lending can be broadly categorized into two:-Secured and unsecured lending[5]. Loans and advances are said to be unsecured when there are no specific collateral pledged. This form of lending is mostly given to blue chips company (ies) with better credit rating, good reputation and ability to generate cash flow etc while secured loans are loans that are attached to specific collateral pledged.

Bank Lending is embedded in certain canon which is popularly called the 5C's- Character, Capacity, Cash, Collateral and Conditions[6] and the PARTS- Purpose, Amount, Repayments, Tenor and Security[7].

1.2 Cannons of Bank Lending

1.2.1 Character

This first canon has to do with the borrower's credit history. Is it good or bad? That is does he or she has a good record of repaying debts. This also bows down to affect the borrower's integrity. Information relating to credit history of borrowers is usually obtained from credit bureau agencies as their reports indicates the number of customer borrowing accounts and their respective exposures in all financial institution whether performing or not. A review of such report will determine whether the customer is credit worthy or not.

1.2.2 Capacity

This cannon dwell on the borrower's ability to repay the loan. This is done by accessing the customer income against debt. That is debt to income ratio is used. In addition, it also looks at the legal status of the borrower; is he or she a minor and if it's a company, are they empowered by their memorandum and article of association (MERMART) to borrow. If it's a partnership, is their partnership deed support it or not and if yes, who authorize to borrow on behalf of the partner.

---

[5] John E. I . "Practice of Banking" CIBN *Exam Distance Learning Pack.* PE III.. Accountancy Training and Publication Ltd. Lagos 2011. Pp. 125-147

[6] http://www.investopedia.com/terms/f/five-c-credit.asp. Retrieved.25/12/2015. 5:26pm

[7] Amateur Economist" *Lending Mnemonic"* (2011); Available at http://theamateurecom.blogspot.com/2011/10/Lending_mnemonic.html. Retrieved 13/07/2015. 4:53pm

1.2.3 Capital

Under this canon, the stake or equity of the borrower on this business to be financed is also taking into cognizance because a large contribution by the borrower decreases the chance of default and vice versa. The cannon also cover the business cash flow. Can the business to be financed able to generate inflows enough to service the loan?

1.2.4 Collateral

This cannon ensure commitment on the part of the borrower as it is considered as the seat belt in case default situation. Under this arrangement, the borrower has to pledge an asset against the loan and advances. Therefore, it is pertinent that such asset must be important to the borrower that he or she cannot afford to lose. Consequently, it make the borrower to be committed towards the loan and if there is default the bank can go ahead to sell off the said asset and recovery the outstanding balances of the loan.

1.2.5 Condition

This canon is very versatile as it covers a lot of issues surrounding credit and that is why control has been carved out of it which some literatures consider it as 6 Cs of credit. Condition dwells on how the borrowers intend to use the money, its current market share and the expected market share, competitive advantage, climate for customer products, sensitivity to change in business condition, labour market condition in the industry, impact of inflation, applicable banking law and documentation etc.

However, apart from the 5cs of credit, there exist other acronyms banks used as a guide in credit lending and analysis[8].

i. **PARTS:** Purpose, Amount, Repayment, Terms and Security.

ii. **CAMPARI**: Character, Ability, Margin, Purpose, Amount, Repayment, Insurance (Security)

iii. **CCCPARTS:** Character, Capacity, Repayment, Capital, Purpose, Amount, Repayment, Terms and Security.

iv. **PARSER:** Person, Amount, Repayment, Security, Expediency and Remuneration

After considering, the first aid tool kits that are used in credit lending and analysis we shall consider some of the major lending products of commercial banks.

---

[8] John E. I . "Practice of Banking" CIBN *Exam Distance Learning Pack.* PE III.. Accountancy Training and Publication Ltd. Lagos 2011. Pp. 125-147

Chapter Two: Conventional Bank Lending Products

2.0 Introduction

Conventional banks in its bid to actively perform their role as financial intermediation. i.e. mobilizing funds from surplus areas to deficit area develop certain products that can aid such drive. The major products that are required by conventional banks to effectively channel funds to deficit areas are as thus; overdraft, Import and Export Finance Facility, LC Confirmation Line, Invoice Discounting facility, Local Purchase order, Term loan lease etc.

2.1 Overdraft

This is a kind of short term credit facility with maximum tenor of 12 months that allows customer to continue to withdraw money from his or her account even if it is not funded up to a specified approved limit. It can also be called different nomenclature depending upon the bank concern. It could be refer to as temporary overdraft (TOD)

Overdraft is usually applicable to current account holders, though some hybrid saving savings account can also enjoy such benefit but depending on the banks policy regarding to credit. It is mostly used to augment working capital of the borrowers and its repayment source is usually from proceeds from sales or realization of the pledged collateral in case of default.

In addition, overdraft can be single or revolving in nature. It is single because it is one-off and it is revolving because it has the option of rollover. This form of credit is usually associated with a risk of possible diversion. i.e. customer might end up not using the said fund for the actual purpose it was meant for, thus necessitate the need for banks to request for collateral so as to mitigate such risk.

2.2 Import Overdraft

This type of facility is used to finance the expense related to the import such as duty payment, freight and insurance and FX to open letter of Credit. Repayment is usually cash generated from the sales proceeds. Under this type of arrangement to it recommendable the bank process the expense related items directly so as to avoid possible diversion of funds.

2.3 Import Finance Facility

IFF as popularly called amongst bank is a type of credit facility that is used for the financing of importation of industrial goods particularly raw materials and consumable goods with a maximum tenor of one(1) year. It is pertinent to note that such goods must not be contraband, must be readily disposable locally, must have a life span of less than 270days

This form of facility is targeted at Multi-National Companies (MNC's), Large SME's involved in manufacturing, oil and gas, import and export companies etc. under this arrangement, the borrower contributes equity which is usually 30% of the total amount which on the whole, the payment is done via Letter of Credit. There is also a warehouse arrangement which is usually tripartite (Bank, warehouse agent and borrower). Upon delivery, the goods are warehoused which is to be realized in piecemeal to the borrower depending on the progress report but this is mostly applicable if the borrower has not pledged any collateral.

The security arrangement of this kind of facility is lien on the shipping documents, personal guarantee, insurance etc. This type of facility is not free from risk such as exchange rate risk, product risk, market risk, payment risk, regulatory risk and over-invoicing etc

2.4 Export Finance Facility

This facility type is considered as the opposite of Import Finance Facility (IFF). This has to do with the finance to export goods. This goods includes agricultural produce such as cocoa, palm produces rubber etc. this loan is a self liquidating type because it Nils off immediately the export proceeds hits the account whether or not the tenor has expired.

Consequently, the facility tenor per cycle should be matched with the customer export cycle. It is also key that the goods to be exported should be easily assessed for value and quality which is usually done by reputable export testing and inspection services. Arrangement must be made for bond warehousing and the bank must not disburse funds unless the exporter has secured a confirmed irrevocable letter of credit established by the oversee buyer.

2.5 Foreign Currency Loan

This is a foreign currency dominated loan. It could be in USA dollars, pound sterling or Euro. Under such arrangement the pricing is based on London Inter Bank offer rate (LIBOR) and the bank marginal cost of funds etc. Key risk associated with this type of facility is the exchange rate risk.

2.6 Letter of Credit Confirmation Line

Letter of Credit is a document issued by a bank or financial institution to a prospective borrower for an agreed amount and for a definite or indefinite period[9]. This form of credit is usually foreign currency dominated. It is granted to customers to finance their import by utilizing their banks confirmation line with offshore banks.

LC confirmation line is usually granted to highly reliable and banks major customer with adequate security. The pricing of such facility is based at London Inter Bank Offer Rate (LIBOR) plus spread recommended by the local bank. This line can also be Usuance Line or Stand by LC line. It is usuance line if the LC is payable at a determined future after the presentation of the relevant documents and it is stand by LC line as it guarantee of the customer payment by the bank incase or event the customer defaults.

2.7 Invoice Discounting Facility (Receivable Financing)

IDF as it is popularly called is a type of facility where customers are permitted to borrow money based on their invoice. The bank usually finance 70% of the value of the invoices and most at time it is recommended that the contract employer should be amongst the approved list of the banks counter party.

The repayment source of this type of facility is strictly based on receipt of cash on invoice and the security is based on domiciliation of proceeds. Risks associated with such facility are collection risk, diversion risk, non-acceptance of invoice etc.

2.8 Local purchase Order and Contract Finance Facility

LPO and CFF are popular acronyms used to address such facilities. This refers to a type of facilities that is granted to borrower to finance the supply of materials, equipment or execution of a specific supply contract. Under this arrangement, the bank will finance only 70% of the total LPO sum or contract sum upon confirmation of its authenticity while customer contributes 30% which serves as equity.

Repayment of this type of loan is from proceeds of LPO or contract and it is self liquidating because upon receipt of the proceeds it nils off the loan amount whether or not the tenor expires. Security for this type of facility is domiciliation of contract or LPO proceeds and to mitigate against risk it is advisable that bank deals with companies

[9] Hartzell, D. Dictionary of Management. Ogun. Melrose Books and Publishing, 2011. P.229

on their approved list of counterparties. Risks associated with this type of facility are performance risk, collection risk and diversion risk etc.

2.9 Term Loan

This type of loan is considered as long term in nature. i.e it can be medium based (3-5yrs) or long-term based-above 5years. This is a type of loan that is used to finance specific fixed asset or investment. Under this arrangement, the repayment source is dependent on the cash flow generated from the business or the usage of the asset. The repayment can be either equally or unequal which can be monthly, quarterly, semi-quarterly annually etc.

Taking into cognizance, the complexities involved in this type of loan such as the exposures and time etc key issues such as the purpose, company key personnel, quality of management, profitability of the business, cash flow, quality of collateral risk-business, regulatory and environmental risk needs to be addressed.

2.10 Direct Credit or Drawing against Uncleared Effect (DAUE)

This is a type of overdraft credit facility which permit customer to access proceed of a cheque or draft drawn on other banks before it is been cleared. This type of credit is avail to customer with proven integrity. The key risk associated with such facility is return risk. i.e if such cheque is returned.

2.11 Leases

Lease is a contract between the owner of the asset (Lessor) and the user (lessee) whereby the former grants the latter the right to use the asset for a payment of rentals over an agreed period of time. Lease can be Finance or operating lease. Finance lease is also known as full payout lease. It is a type where in the lessor transfers substantially all the risk and reward related to lessee. Operating lease is where the risk and reward are not transferred to the lessee.[10]

Under this arrangement, the borrower is expected to contribute a minimum of 20-30% of the value of asset to be financed while the bank finances the outstanding balances. Security under this type of facility is usually the item financed, though the title of pit is in the name of the bank, thus gives the bank the proprietary right while the borrower has the possessory right. Other security is comprehensive insurance on asset which the interest of the bank will be noted as first loss payee.

[10] www.efinancemangment.com/typeslease.Retrieved on 23/03/2017. 10:00am

2.12 Loan Syndication

This refers to as a lending practice or arrangement in which one bank is unable to grant a loan to a large borrower because of legal or internal limits invites other banks to participate in providing the required credit facility[11]. This is mostly used for financing elephant projects. Repayment source are usually from the cash flow generated by the business.

Under this form of lending, parties involves are large borrower, lead bank (Syndicate manager) and participating bank. All lenders will have equal right and duties in such transaction on a pro-rata basis.

2.13 Specialized Loan

The following loans are considered to be specialized according to the CBN Prudential Guideline for Deposit Money Banks in Nigeria[12]:-

2.13.1 Agricultural Finance

This constitutes loans granted for agricultural purposes. It can be farm credit or non farm credit. Farm credit includes production loan for inputs like seeds, fertilizer, farm development finance and purchase of agricultural equipment etc. Non farm credit includes financing for livestock such as diary, poultry and fisheries etc.

Although, commercial banks tend to have little concern in financing this type of facility due to its kind of risk and that is why the Central Bank have energize existing intervention funds like Agricultural Credit Guarantee Scheme Fund (ACGSF), Commercial Agriculture Credit Scheme (CACS) and developed new intervention funds such as Anchor Borrowers scheme etc in 2015 so as that commercial bank can freely used such funds to finance the sector.

2.13.2 Mortgage Loan

This type of loan is used for the financing of purchase of new or improvement of real estate property. It is normally a long term loan that has tenor of above 5years. Though, the tenor varies according to banks policy. Under this arrangement the borrower is expected to contribute between 20-30% of the property value while the bank finances the outstanding amount.

---

[11]Onyiriuba Leo . *Analysing and Managing Risk of Bank Lending*. NFS Data Bureau Ltd. Lagos Second Edition. 2008. P. 373
[12] Central Bank of Nigeria (2010). Prudentials Guidelines for Deposit Money Bankss in Nigeria. P. 9-11

Repayment source can be from salary source or sales generated from the business and it can be repayable monthly, quarterly etc. security for this type of lending is usually the property financed as the title of the property will be with the borrower-legal mortgage will be taken over property. Other securities will be insurance over property with the banks interest noted as first loss payee, personal guarantee etc.

2.13.3 Margin Loan

This is a type of loan that enables a borrower to finance against shares. The term margin refers to the difference between the market value of the shares and the cost of the shares. Under this arrangement, the source of repayment is from proceeds of sales of such shares and also the same shares is been used as a security.

2.13.4 Object Finance

It is a credit facility that is used to finance the acquisition of physical asset such as ship, aircrafts, fleet etc. The repayment sources largely depend on the inflow generated by the asset. Security for such type of lending is usually the asset financed.

2.13.5 Project Finance

It is in form of non-recourse or limited recourse financing where by the lender based their credit decision solely or primarily on the cash flow of the project with respect to the repayment of the project debt. Thus, the project should be capable of servicing itself.

2.13.6 Real Estate Loan

It is called Income producing real estate. This is a type of loan meant for the financing of real estate (office building, shopping mall, residential buildings, hostels etc). Repayment source is primarily cash inflow from the real estate and legal mortgage is usually taken as the security. This type of facility can also be in form of Commercial Real Estate loan. This is considered as high volatility commercial real estate.

Under this type of loan, the banks considers the collateral, credit worthiness of the borrower, financial statement (3-5yrs) and other financial ratios such loan to value ratio and debt-service coverage ratio.[13]

2.13.7 SME Loan

This is a type of loan that is meant for the financing of Small and Medium Scale enterprises. SME is defined as any manufacturing enterprise with an asset base of between N5M –N500M (excluding land) and labour force of between

[13] www.investopedia.com/c/commercial-real-estate-loan.asp. Retrieved on 26/03/2017. 3:30pm

11 and 300.[14] For instance in order to support this form of financing because the conventional banks were not doing enough, the Central Bank has introduced intervention fund in 2010 such as the Small and Medium Enterprises Credit Guarantee Scheme (SMECGS) Micro, Small and Medium Scale Enterprises Fund.

2.14 Consumer (Retail) Loan

Loans under this category are mostly meant for salary earned individuals who require such to solve their urgent personal, family or household needs. Example of such are:-

2.14.1 Salary Advance

This type of credit facility is given to individuals in advance before their salary is been paid. It is normally a one-off facility with a maximum tenor of 30days. The beneficiary can only have access to 50% of his or her salary. Security is usually domiciliation of salary and gratuities.

2.14.2 Personal Loan

Under this credit facility type, loan is availed to the individual to attend to some urgent personal needs such as medical bills, house rents etc. it has a tenor of 3 -5years in some instances depending on the banks credit policy.

Under this arrangement, the maximum obligor limit is determined by 33.33% of the borrowers take home pay. Repayment source of such facility is mostly based on salary where as the Security is usually domiciliation of salary and gratuities and in some cases personal guarantee is also required

2.14.3 Home Appliances Loan

This is a type of loan meant for the purchase of electronics, laptops, house hold asset etc. Under this arrangement, the maximum obligor limit is determined by 33.33% of the borrowers take home pay. Repayment source of such facility is mostly based on salary.

Performa invoice from the bank approved list of vendors is required to enable the bank process such facility which will also be confirmed to ascertain its authenticity and alongside other relevant documents. Asset finance will be in the banks name and upon full payment it will be reversed to the borrower's name. Security required for this credit type is usually domiciliation of salary and gratuities, title of the asset financed, insurance policy and in some cases personal guarantee are also required.

[14] CBN (2010)" N200B Small and Medium Enterprises (SME) Credit Guarantee Scheme (SMECGS)" Available at: https://www.cbn.gov.ng>guidelines>dfd/pdf

2.14.4 Education Loan

This facility type is used to finance the payment of school fees and payment of professional examination. The tenor of the credit type is usually 23 months. Under this arrangement, the borrower is expected to contribute at least 20% as equity while the bank finances the outstanding balances. . Under this arrangement, the maximum obligor limit is determined by 33.33% of the borrowers take home pay. Repayment source of such facility is mostly based on salary.

2.14.5 Auto loan

Auto loan is a type of loan that is used to finance the purchase of car mostly brand new cars. This facility has a tenor of 3-5years depending on the car type (Korean or Japan) and the credit policy of the bank. Under this arrangement, the maximum obligor limit is determined by 33.33% of the borrowers take home pay. Repayment source of such facility is mostly based on salary.

Performa invoice from the bank approved list of vendors is required to enable the bank process such facility which will also be confirmed to ascertain its authenticity and alongside other relevant documents. Asset finance will be in the banks name and upon full payment it will be reversed to the borrower's name. Security required for this credit type is usually domiciliation of salary and gratuities, title of the asset financed, insurance policy and in some cases personal guarantee are also required.

2.14.6 Credit Cards

This refers to cards which permits customers to make payment on credit.[15] This is just like the normal debit cards but in this case it has the facility to withdraw or make payment up to certain approved limit. This type of card is issued to customer with proven track record.

In all the credit products operated by the conventional bank, the idea or notion of security (Collateral) cannot be relegated to the background as it is required in one way or the other. Thus we can see collateral as a sufficient condition towards lending after considering all other necessary condition such as the character, capacity etc of the borrower.

[15] Central Bank of Nigeria (2010). Prudential's Guidelines for Deposit Money Banks in Nigeria. P. 8

Chapter Three: Overview of Bank Securities (Collateral)

3.0 Introduction

In all the canons mentioned, security has been included which implies that security should be highly considered when lending which makes the secured form of lending preferable.

Apart from security (collateral) been part of the canon of lending, the statutory regulations has also stressed about taking security against loans and advances. For instance, in Nigeria the Bank and other Financial Institutions Decree (BOFIA), section 18 (1) provides that no manager or any other officer of a bank shall inter alia

"Grant any advance, loan or credit facility to any person, unless it is authorised in accordance with the rules and regulations of the bank and where adequate security is required by such rules and regulations such security shall, prior to the grant, be obtained for the advances, loan or credit facility and shall be deposited with the bank"

In order to ensure compliance of the above clause as stated above, subsection 2 stipulates that

"Any contravention of this provision is made an offence for which the manager or officer concerned is liable to a fee of N100,000 or to imprisonment for a term of 3years. In addition, any gains or benefit accruing to any such person so convicted shall be forfeited to the FGN".

Although, for banks to continue to be in the business of lending and to meet best practices they continue to develop and review their internal rules and regulations on its lending so also complying with external regulations which is encapsulated in its documents called credit policy. This policy documents address key issues such as type of customer, credit size, quality of security, risk consideration, type of industry and business etc but one fact remains that with all this measures put in place, one cannot absolutely resolve that no loan will go bad because the operations of bank has already factor in such possibility as it operates based on the probability theories. Thus, bad loan can only be minimized.

In order to minimize the risk of loans going bad, the only life support system is Security (collateral) which is also seen as a seat belt to lending and the last resort towards recovering bad loans by banks. In lieu of that, the definition of security in this context cannot be relegated to the background.

3.1 Definition of Security (Collateral)

The concept security has different meanings to different persons or professions. Literally, security is defined as thus;

a. The activities involved in protecting a country, building or person against attack, danger etc.

b. The state of feeling happy and safe from danger or worry.

c. A valuable item such as house that you agree to give to somebody if you are unable to pay back the money that you have borrowed from them.

d. Documents proving that somebody is the owner of shares etc in a particular company.[16]

From the above, definitions (c) best relates to our topic. Security refers to an insurance against unforeseen developments and the last source through which the bank can get its money recouped should things turns sour[17]. Igweike (2004) define security as simply means something given or received to ensure that certain obligation owed by the person giving it to the person receiving it is fulfilled[18].

Sykes (1972) sees security as a transaction whereby a person to whom an obligation is owed by another person called the debtor is afforded in addition to the personal promise of the debtor to discharge the obligations, rights exercisable against some property of the debtor in order to discharge the obligation[19].

Security has occupied series of vacuums in the arena of bank lending business because the collection of this security does not immediately implies that the bank will immediately sell it but to ensure some level of commitment from the customer in order to meet up its obligations. That is why it is very recommendable to receive collaterals that are very prime to the borrower which cannot afford to lose.

Security in lending has been classified into three (3) as follows; [20]:-

i. Proprietary Security: - A security is said to be proprietary whereby the title in the subject matter of the security is passed from the debtor to the creditor. As in the case of a mortgage where the title in the landed property is passed to the mortgagee by the mortgagor.

ii. Possessory Security: - A security is said to be possessory if there is a transfer of possession in the subject matter of the security from the debtor to the creditor. For example, where a pledge or pawn is taken as security.

iii. Security that have neither proprietary nor possessory transfer, but a mere appropriation of interest in the subject matter of the security. For instance charge or hypothecation.

Having dealt with the classification of security, it is also pertinent to note that for banks to continue to collect security against loans and advances, such security must possess certain attributes.

---

[16] Hornby A. S. *Oxford Advanced Learners Dictionary*. Oxford University Press. USA 7th Edition, 2006: Pp. 1320, 1321
[17] Afolabi, Layi .*Law and Practice of Banking*. Heinemann Educational books Nig. Ibadan 1999: P.210
[18] Igweike, K. I. Law of Banking and Negotiable Instruments. Africana First Press Limited.Lagos.2004.P.170
[19] Onyiriuba Leo . *Analysing and Managing Risk of Bank Lending*. NFS Data Bureau Ltd. Lagos Second Edition. 2008. P. 373
[20] *Halliday Vs Holgate(1868)LR3 Exch.p.299 at 302. In* Onyiriuba Leo(2008) . *Analysing and Managing Risk of Bank Lending*. NFS Data Bureau Ltd. Lagos Second Edition. 2008. P. 373

3.2 Features of Security (Collateral)

There exist certain distinct features of security which serves as a first aid guide or information to banks when collecting securities from borrowers. Prominent amongst such features are as follows:-

a. **Title**: Title refers as "the legal right to own something"[21]. Thus, a security must have good title which is free from encumbrances or encroachment. In order to authenticate such title, banks are to conduct an independent legal search from land registry in case of landed properties because lending against security with a bad title is a kind of unsecured lending invariably nursing bad debt as the bank stands the risk of losing such security in case of default during realization.

b. **Adequacy or Sufficiency in Value:** A good security must be adequate or sufficient to cover the bank exposure because accepting a security which is below the facility amount is as good as creating some part of the facility unsecured. In lieu of this, most banks normally takes the force sale value (FSV) as against the market value in case of landed properties, the surrender value in case of insurance policy. In order to ensure adequate margin in the security, banks creates a bench mark that the security will satisfy before been accepted. This benchmark varies according to banks various policy. For instance, some might be 150% of the force sale value (FSV).

c. **Stability in Value:** A good security must have a stable or increasing market value. This feature is very important at the instance of realizing the asset or properties in case of default. Accepting a security that has a decreasing value will jeopardize the facility. For instance accepting landed properties in urban areas is highly preferable than accepting same properties in a rural area because such properties in urban area has a stable and increasing value *ceteris paribus*. In a similar vein, a good security should have a basis or standard of valuation. That is it should be a something that can be easily valued objectively rather than using intuition.

d. **Realizable:** This attributes form one of the key basis of security because it is part of the recovery option in case of default. This implies that a good security must be easily realizable without exorbitant cost or delay but this can be achieved if there exist a ready market. For instance, accepting landed properties in the rural areas, its realization will be delayed because no one will be interested in buying such properties in such location and also accepting shares of a private company will be difficult to realize because it is not traded on the floor of the stock exchange and the restriction on its MERMART.

[21] Hornby A. S. *Oxford Advanced Learners Dictionary*. Oxford University Press. USA 7th Edition, 2006. P. 1554

e. **Transferability or Assignment:** This means "that your property or rights now belongs to somebody else"[22]. In lieu of that, a good security should be easily assigned and re-assigned. By the assignment we are taking into cognizance the security interest- right given to one party on the asset of the another party to secure the performance of an obligation[23]. In Nigeria, for instance the shares of a private company cannot be easily assigned or transferred due to the restriction on its Memorandum and Article of association (MEMERT) and the CAMA Act of 1990.

f. **Acceptable by law:** A good security must also be acceptable by the law of the land and not prohibited. In essence, all the dynamics involved in accepting a security must be legal binding and enforceable by law so as to take care of situation where there is a breach of the terms and conditions of the contract, the court can easily redressed such. For instance, the popular Ajilo case. That is Savannah bank of Nigeria Limited and D.B Orisan Vs Ammel O. Ajilo and Ammelo Photo industries Limited (1989) can also bear testimony to this fact[24].

3.3 Benefits of Security

There is no gain saying that there exist no benefit in accepting or collecting security against loans and advances because relying on the commitment of the promise to pay as when due which is the usual language of the debtor (borrower) is not enough as any default in such loans will lead to the depletion of share holders funds which invariably affects the profit position of such banks if such bad loans are to be written off but when there are security pledge the bank will at least recover substantial part of its exposure.

However, the rationale behind taking security against loans and advances is to take care of the future because lending to the various economic units (Individuals, organization and government) has to do with the future performance of such loan able funds in turning around the business fortunes but, there exist situations which is beyond control and thus, has a negative effect on the business such as depression, recession, decline in market demand etc which will invariably affects the repayment of such loans.

The benefits of accepting security against loans and advances can be summarized as follows below:-

---

[22] Hornby A. S. *Oxford Advanced Learners Dictionary*. Oxford University Press. USA 7th Edition, 2006. P.75

[23] R.M Goode in Onyiriuba Leo . *Analysing and Managing Risk of Bank Lending*. NFS Data Bureau Ltd. Lagos Second Edition. 2008

[24] Afolabi, Layi .*Law and Practice of Banking*. Heinemann Educational books Nig. Ibadan 1999

a. **Minimization of Risks:** Risks refers to as the form of uncertainty while the actual outcome of an action is not known[25]. However taking security against loans and advances will greatly reduce the risk the bank is bound to encounter be it credit risk, liquidity risk etc but if such loans are availed on the basis of mere promise to repay as at when due, the bank is at the mercy of the borrower as the risk of such will be high on the part of the bank in case of default.

b. **Increases borrowers commitment:** Taking security by banks further creates a high sense of commitment on the part of the borrower because he may not want to lose his or her property. In this case he has a stake in the business of lending and he may not want to play in any form that may jeopardize the loan. But if there are no securities against such lending, it will be disastrous on the part of the bank as the borrower has nothing to lose; hence his commitment will be low.

c. **Creditor's interest highly safeguard in case of liquidation:** Liquidation refers to the process of closing down a business and disposing of its assets. In case of liquidation, the creditor is in a preferred position if security is pledge against the loans and advances collected by the individual or company and that is why it is highly recommended that all the necessary documents required are collected, duly executed and perfected.

The preferred position of the creditor is further enforced by the CAMA act of 1990, which stipulates that the asset of the company are to be applied in the order of priority; 1. Fixed charge holders 2. Liquidation expenses 3. Preferential claims 4. Floating charge holders 5. Unsecured creditors 6. Amount due to members e.g. Dividend 7. Repayment of capital according to the class priority.

Based on the order of priority it is evident that fixed charge holders or secured creditors are rated first and while unsecured creditors are rated fifth. This depicts how the creditor interest is highly protected and safeguarded, thus the need for collecting collateral cannot be relegated to the background.

d. **Minimizes inside related credits:** According to the CBN prudential guidelines for Deposit Money banks in Nigeria (2010) 3.4 (c) see insiders are includes directors, significant shareholders and employees while the BOFIA act defines the term directors are includes directors' wife, husbands, fathers, mothers, brothers, sisters, sons, daughter and their spouses.

Thus inside- related credits are credit availed to the aforementioned. However, security against loans and advances helps to ensure that insider related credits are not abused invariably controls the excessiveness of most directors.

[25] Black . J (2002). *Oxford Dictionary of Economics*. USA. Oxford University press. P.406

e. **Gives Creditor the Right to Sue:** Security taken against loans and advances gives the creditor the right to take legal action in case of default. This is seen as amongst a popular recovery options available to the credit And that is why it is highly recommended that such security should be structured in a manner that it should be legally binding on both parties which must be supported by collecting, executing all the required documents before disbursement.

However, this benefit is lost if the process required by law is not duly followed. Amongst such mistakes banks do are not seeking governor's consent, not registering of such deeds and stamping, error in documentation etc. failure to perfect these securities will result to failure of the right to sue because the bank will have no basis for defense.

f. **Fulfils Psychological sense of Comfort:** Taking security against loans and advances fulfils the creditors' psychological sense of comfort. That is it tends to fulfill the ego of the transactions as every parties involved mindset will be a little bit fulfilled. Man by its nature has the fear of unknown and coupled with the fact that life is full of uncertainty so by collecting security that fear has been minimize to some extent because there is a fall back no matter which side of the uncertainty that may occurred.

Chapter Four: Acceptable Forms of Conventional Bank Securities (Collateral)

4.0 Introduction

There are different types of securities (Collateral) conventional banks accepts from their customer in term of loan and advances. This type of securities also varies according to their various loan products which is clearly defined in their credit policy documents. Though, we are going to consider the major types of securities that are common to all conventional banks.

4.1 Land as a Security

Land as a security does not only refer to the surface of the land but to all gifts of nature such as rivers, oceans, climate, mountains, fishes, mines forest etc. lands refers to materials and forces which nature gives freely for mans aid, in land, water, in air, light and heat[26]. The land use act of 1978, defines land in the context of physical improvement in the nature of road improvement, services, water, electricity, drainage, building structures or such improvement that may enhance the value of the land for industrial, agricultural and residential purpose[27].

Land is considered as an old form of security against loans and advances that it has stand the taste of time because it is still considered amongst the best and reliable form of securities.

4.1.1 Types of Land

Land can be categorized into four (4) different types[28] according to its nature and title. Developed and undeveloped land according to its nature while registered and unregistered land according to its title.

[26] Alfred Marshall. Principles of Economics. Great Mind Series. 1890

[27] Section 50(1)

[28] Afolabi, Layi .*Law and Practice of Banking*. Heinemann Educational books Nig. Ibadan 1999. P.309

4.1.1.1 Developed Land

Developed land refers to a land where there exist physical improvements in the nature of road improvement, services, water, electricity, drainage, building structures or such improvement that may enhance the value of the land for industrial, agricultural and residential purpose.

Thus any land without physical improvements as mentioned above cannot be referred to as a developed land. This form of land is considered suitable for security against any loan or advances as it has more value due to its improvements made on it.

4.1.1.2 Undeveloped Land

This is the opposite or reverse of developed land. An undeveloped land can be refer to as land without any physical improvement in whatever form as cited in section 50 (1). This form of land is not acceptable as a form of security by banks because the value of any land lies on the improvements made on such land even if such land is registered.

4.1.1.3 Registered Land

A land is said to be registered if the interest in the land is duly registered at land registry. For instance in Nigeria such interest in the land is fully created by the state governors[29]. This is evidenced by the issuance of certificate of occupancy which is expected to be registered with 6months of issuance. It is usually for a period of 99years for Nigerians and 50 years for non-Nigerians.

However, there are interest in land created before the promulgation of the Land use act by way of ordinary receipt, conveyance, assignment etc but such interest was incorporated in the act as stipulated in Section 34(2) which they now have an automatic statutory of occupancy.

4.1.1.4 Unregistered Land

This is a type of land whose interest is not registered at the land registry. This type of land is not usually acceptable as a form of security because the title or interest of such a land is ambiguous; investigation of title of such land in order to verify the authenticity of its title will be difficult. This will make the transfer of the said title from the mortgagor to the mortgagee a problem.

However, there exist certain conditions or factors that are needed to be taken into consideration before accepting such land as a security against loans and advances in whatever form. Prominent among such factors are:-

i. The borrowers' must have good title to the land and registered at the land registry

[29] Nigeria Land Use act 1978.Part 1, Section 1

ii. It must be free from any existing charge or encumbrances

iii. It must be of commercial value

iv. The Force Sale value (FSV) must be taken into consideration with margins rather than the Market value which should be done by a qualified estate valuer.

Year in year out, in the business of lending engaged by banks and other financial institutions, land is considered amongst the best form of security but this prompt a question. What are the reasons responsible for this? Amongst such reasons are as follows:-

i. The value of land is relatively stable as it is the only fixed asset that appreciates rather than depreciates.

ii. The title of the land can be easily investigated via land registry whether or not there are existing charges or the title is genuine and any other relevant information can also be obtained. This is usually conducted by an independent lawyer.

iii. It is immovable from one place to another even if the debtor has a possessory interest over it. Hence he cannot hide the security in case of default.

iv. The value of it can be easily ascertained even if an absolute value cannot be obtained by different estate valuers.

v. It is marketable any time most especially if the land is located in a very good location.

vi. It is an asset that people cherish and hold at a high esteemed and cannot afford to lose in any circumstance

vii. It has a legal backing or support. Thus it is legally binding on both the creditor and debtor.

Despite its success in penetrating the financial world, it is not free from certain shortcomings. Amongst which are:-

i. If the land is not located in a good location, realizing or selling it will be difficult.

ii. The entire process from searching, valuation, perfection etc is expensive and time consuming.

iii. The debtor may end up intentionally or unintentionally putting the property in a bad condition which may affect the value of the property.

iv. Revocation of Certificate of occupancy by government and poor compensation.

v. Property could be destroyed by act of God such as flood, land slide or earthquake.

vi. Overvaluation of the property by the estate valuers.

vii. In case of fire outbreak on the property, there is usually a delay in settlement of claims by insurance companies and that is why banks prefer using their subsidiary for insurance policy.

Accepting land as a form of security against loans and advances by banks and other financial institutions implies that a mortgage must be created or taken on the property which is popularly called Mortgage of Real property.

4.1.2 Mortgage

Mortgage refers to a loan using a real asset such as house or other building as collateral[30]. The concept is a term derived from two (2) old French words "*Mort*" (from Latin *mortuus* "dead") and " *Gage*" meaning Dead pledge[31]. Mortgage can be seen as a legal or equitable conveyance of title as a security for the payment of debt or the discharge of some other obligation for which it is given subject to a condition that the title shall be re-conveyed if the mortgage debt is liquidated[32]

However, in order to create mortgage the legal capacity of all the parties involved has to be taken into consideration, just like a contract. Amongst such things to be considered is that the mortgagor and mortgagee must not be an infant, must not be drunken at the point of consummating the transaction or be an insane person and if it is a corporation, then it has to be permitted by it Memorandum and Article of Association(MEMART)

4.1.2.1 Forms of Mortgage

Mortgage is basically made of two (2) different forms namely; Simple mortgage and third party mortgage

4.1.2.1.1 Simple Mortgage

In this form of mortgage, two (2) parties are only involved- Mortgagor and Mortgagee. It is created when the borrower directly mortgages his/her land properties to the lender. Under this arrangement, there exist a particular standard Deed forms which is to be executed and adopted by the mortgagor as it cannot be used interchangeably with that of tripartite forms.

4.1.2.1.2 Third Party Mortgage

This is also called tripartite mortgage because three (3) parties are involved; the Bank, borrower and the mortgagor. This is a type of mortgage where by a third party pledges his or her property on behalf of a borrower.

---

30 Black. J (2002). *Oxford Dictionary of Economics*. USA. Oxford University press. P.309

31 https://www.merriam-webster.com/dictionary/mortgage.Retrived 15/03/2017. 6:24am

32 Lord Lindley, M.R in Stanley Vs Wilde (1899). Chap 474 adopted. In practical approach to law of real property in Nigeria by I.O.Smith. p.36

This form of mortgage is mostly found amongst companies where the directors use their personal properties as surety to enable the company borrow from such banks and that is, if such company does not has properties in his own name. Deed of tripartite legal mortgage forms is usually executed under this form of mortgage.

4.1.2.2 Nature of Mortgages

Mortgages can be created in two (2) ways which is as follows: Legal Mortgages and Equitable Mortgages.

4.1.2.2.1 Legal Mortgage

This refers to the transfer or conveyance of the whole interest of the mortgagor in real estate to the mortgagee by a deed of mortgage duly stamped, registered and the Governor consent duly obtained to the transaction[33].

Under this arrangement, the proprietary interest is transferred to the mortgagee (the bank) by the mortgagor (borrower) until such debt is paid back before it will be reassigned back to the mortgagor. In this case, the mortgagee still holds the possessory interest of the said property. This form of mortgage is highly recommended as both parties are in a safe position

4.1.2.2.3 Advantages of Legal Mortgage

The advantages of legal mortgage are as follows:

i. The mortgagee the right to sell the landed properties without hindrance or constraints from the mortgagor in as far as it is duly perfected.

ii. Court order is not required in case of realization as required as obtain in the case of equitable mortgage.

iii. Legal mortgage has priority over equitable mortgage during liquidation even if it was created without any prior knowledge of any charge.

iv. It is the safest type of mortgage a lender can obtain if its process is duly followed and complied with.

---

[33] Onyiriuba Leo . *Analysing and Managing Risk of Bank Lending*. NFS Data Bureau Ltd. Lagos Second Edition. 2008. P. 373

v. Legal mortgage is created by deed and upon defaults all remedies available to the mortgagee is automatically invoked.

4.1.2.2.4 Disadvantages of Legal Mortgage

Despite its advantages, it is not free from its short comings. Below are some of the disadvantages of legal mortgage:-

i. Difficulty in obtaining Governors consent. For example, in Nigeria the land use act (1978), Section 21 and 22 provides that it shall not be lawful for any customary right of occupancy or any part thereof to be alienated by assignment, mortgage or transfer possession, sub lease without the consent of the Governor but the major problem is obtaining such consent.

ii. Cost Implication: Creation of legal mortgage is very expensive as each steps ranging from investigation of title, valuation up to stamping and registration of such deeds an expense is been incurred.

iii. The process involves in creating legal mortgage is cumbersome as it involved a lot of documentary requirements which in most cases are technical.

iv. Creation of legal mortgage is time consuming as it involves different steps and procedures.

4.1.2.3 Documentary Requirements

In Nigeria, to create a legal mortgage over landed properties, it requires the provision of certain documents[34] which is as follows:

i. Original title documents of the property. It can be original Certificate of Occupancy, Deed of Assignment and Deed of Conveyance duly stamp and register.

ii. Three (3) years Tax Clearance Certificate (TCC) of the mortgagor if it is an individual but if it is a company, the company's Tax Clearance Certificate and that of its directors (2) is required.

[34] Onyiriuba Leo . *Analysing and Managing Risk of Bank Lending*. NFS Data Bureau Ltd. Lagos Second Edition. 2008. P. 373; Enterprise Bank Limited, Credit Policy Manual, Feb,2012. P.56

iii. Duly Executed Deed of legal mortgage which can be either a simple or tripartite deed depending on the nature of the transaction.

iv. Receipt of payment of ground rent, tenement rates, development levy, PAYE for the preceding 3 years.

v. Governors Consent to mortgage and in Lagos area Land Form 1c is executed which can suffice also.

vi. Board resolution authorizing the creation of such mortgage in case of a limited liability Company

vii. Copy of Certificate of Incorporation in case of a limited liability Company

viii. Copy of Article and Memorandum of Association in case of a limited liability Company

ix. Insurance policy on the property with the banks interest noted as first loss payee.

x. Copy of an Independent Legal search report which is to be carried out by the banks accredited lawyer.

xi. Copy of a professional valuation report which is to be carried out by the banks accredited lawyer.

xii. Copy of Site plan showing the beacons and approved building plan.

xiii. Passport photograph of the mortgagor.

xiv. Evidence of payment of Neighbourhood Improvement Charge (NIC) (if applicable)

xv. Federal Housing Authority (FHA) Consent Letter to mortgage the property (after due application for consent by the surety) (applicable to FHA and LSDPC properties)

xvi. Confirmation Letter from New Town Development Authority (NTDA)

4.1.2.3 Perfection of a Legal Mortgage

A legal mortgage is said to be perfected in Nigeria, if the following process is duly followed and compiled with.

i. The Governor's consent is been sought and obtained as required by the land use act of 1978, section 22. Failure to comply with use clause makes such a mortgage illegal or null and void. The popular Ajilo case i.e. Savannah bank Nigeria limited and D. B Onu Orisan Vs Ammel O. Ajilo and Ammel photos industries limited (1989) can be used to buttress this point.

ii. The mortgage must be duly stamped as required by the stamp duty act section 86 (1) and 80(3). This normally attracts the Ad volorem duty as provided in section 22 that "An unstamped assignment confers no right on the assignee or his personal representative to sue for the policy.

iii. The mortgage must also be registered as provided in section 2 of land registration act of 1924 because if it is not registered, any mortgage created after it will have priority over it. Such registration should be carried out at the land registry and also if the mortgagor is a company, it should be registered at the Corporate Affairs commission.

4.1.2.2.2 Equitable Mortgage

An equitable mortgage is one which is lacking one or more formalities of legal requirements such as stamping, filing or registration[35]. It is also considered as unregistered mortgage.

This form of mortgage is not a good form of security and that is why in most cases it is advisable for the mortgagee to collect all the required documents for the creation of legal mortgage so as to guard against issues that may likely arise if the mortgagee defaults. Thus, this type of mortgage should be kept at the perfection stage.

However, equitable mortgage can be created in the following ways[36]:-

i. By simple deposit of title documents without execution of memorandum of deposit.

ii. By simple deposit of title documents accompanied by execution of memorandum of deposit

iii. By simple deposit of title documents accompanied by execution of memorandum of deposit and power of attorney.

iv. It can also be created by operation of law. For instance if there is a default or loopholes in the creation of such legal mortgage as obtained in the case of Savannah Bank of Nigeria Vs Ajilo[37]

Under this form of mortgage, execution of the memorandum of deposit is very paramount as it involves certain covenants which devoid it as a form of safe custody. The covenants are as follows:-

---

[35] UsLegal(2017). Available at https://defination.uslegal.com/e/equitable-mortgage. Retrieved 15/03/2017. 3:20pm

[36] Afolabi, Layi .*Law and Practice of Banking.* Heinemann Educational books Nig. Ibadan 1999. P 310

[37] (1989)INWLR. P.305 in Onyiriuba Leo . *Analysing and Managing Risk of Bank Lending*. NFS Data Bureau Ltd. Lagos Second Edition. 2008. P. 379

i. The documents is deposited with the sole aim to create an equitable mortgage

ii. The depositor undertakes to execute a valid legal mortgage or registered charge as the bank may in future demand.

iii. The property will be insured and kept in good condition.

4.1.2.2.3 Documentary Requirements

The following documents are required for the creation of equitable mortgage by banks in Nigeria:

i. Original title documents of the property. It can be original Certificate of Occupancy, Deed of Assignment and Deed of Conveyance duly stamp and register

ii. Executed memorandum of deposit

iii. Executed power of Attorney

iv. A satisfactory legal search report

v. A caution notice filed with the land registry.

4.1.2.2.4 Advantages of Equitable Mortgage

i. The bank can sue for the debt.

ii. The bank can apply to the court for an order of sale.

iii. It is very easy to collect or create and its process is very simple compared to creation of legal mortgage.

iv. The cost of creating an equitable mortgage is less expensive compared to legal mortgage.

4.1.2.2.5 Disadvantages of Equitable Mortgage

i. There exists a problem of realization in case of default due to protracted court action.

ii. The borrower can also engage in sharp practices by collecting the Certified True Copy (CTC) at the land registry and sell it or mortgage it to another bank.

Mortgage once created, can also be further created which can be in form of a second mortgage or Sub-mortgages.

4.1.2.2.6 Second Mortgage

It is a type of subordinate mortgage made while an original mortgage is still in effect[38]. In a similar vein, a mortgage is called a Second mortgage if a further charge is created on an existing mortgaged property. That is the same title deed or documents is been used to borrow money from more than one bank.

In taking a second mortgage over a property, it is very important that a notice is given to the first mortgagee by the second mortgagee because if no notice is issued to the first mortgage, he may return the title deed back to the customer which is not legally liable if anything goes wrong with the unknown second mortgagee.

Also, it is vital to also ensure that the property has sufficient value or margin taking into consideration the Forced sale Value (FSV) rather than the market value. Under, the second mortgage, mortgage can be created at the same time on the same term but only be owes the title, which is called *Pari-Pasu* mortgage (A Latin phrase meaning equal footing)[39]

However, it is also important that the second mortgage be registered at the land registry despite the fact that the second mortgagee is not in possession of the title documents. The second mortgagee can only gain title to the property upon the discharge of the first mortgage due to full payment of the amount.

4.1.2.2.6.1 Advantages of Second Mortgage

i. The second mortgagee receives the title of the property when the first mortgagee exposure is settled.

ii. Upon default, the excess of the sales proceeds are paid to him after when the exposure of the first mortgagee settled.

[38] Investopedia, (2017) available at www.investopedia.com/term/what is second mortgage.asp. Retrieved on 14/03/2017. 10:32am

[39] Investopedia, (2017) available at www.investopedia.com/term/p/pari-passu.asp Retrieved on 14/03/2017. 10:52am

4.1.2.2.6.2 Disadvantages of Second Mortgage

i. If the value of the property declines, the second mortgagee will suffer more because the first mortgagee will want to settle its exposure first.

ii. There is a problem of realization because the second mortgagee does not have title to it even if the mortgagor defaults.

4.1.2.2.7 Sub-Mortgage

A sub mortgage is an agreement in which a mortgage lender uses a mortgage held by him or her as collateral for his or her own loan[40]. This kind of mortgage is called Mortgage of a Mortgage[41]. A mortgage is called Sub-mortgage if a mortgagee used the mortgage created in his favour as security for its own borrowing. That is when the lender (original mortgagee) borrows money against the security of his mortgage deed.

For instance, if Mr. A borrows money say N2, 000,000 from. Bank C and pledges his house as a collateral against the loan. In this case, the former is the mortgagor (Borrower) while the later is the Mortgagee(Bank) but if the mortgagee uses same charge created in his favour to borrow money from Bank D. Thus, Bank D becomes the sub-Mortgagee while Bank C is the Sub-Mortgagor.

Under such arrangement, the sub-mortgagor must execute the memorandum of deposit and a deed of sub-mortgage which has to be registered at the land registry. This form of mortgage is faced with the problem of realization upon default as in fact it is not advisable for banks to accept such form of mortgage due to the technicalities involved in its creation.

4.1.2.3 Realisation of Mortgage

Realization of mortgage is only prompted or called in when the borrowers defaults in the loan terms and conditions. This is considered as a last resort available to a lender. However, there are various methods involved in realizing

[40] https://definations.uslegal.com/s/submortgage. Retrieved on 10/03/2017. 09:30am

[41] Afolabi, Layi .*Law and Practice of Banking*. Heinemann Educational books Nig. Ibadan 1999. P 314

mortgage. This is embedded in a concept called SAFES which meaning is as thus: **S**- Sue, **A**-appoint a receiver, **F**-Foreclosure, **E**- Enter into possession, **S**- Sell

4.1.2.3.1 Sue

To sue refers to make claim against somebody in court about something that they have said or done to harm him[42]. Under this method of realizing mortgages, the bank (lender) has two options. It is either they sue for the debt or the mortgage because both the former and the later are considered as two separate contracts.

In suing for the debt, the bank is charging the mortgagor on his personal agreement or covenant to repay the facility on the agreed terms and conditions. Though, there are instances where the bank will only sue for the debt alone while ignoring the mortgage and vice versa or apply for the both options available.

4.1.2.3.2 Appoint a Receiver:

A receiver refers to a person appointed or chosen by a court to be in charge of a company that is bankrupt[43]. In this case, the bank has the right to appoint a receiver to collect rents or profits accruing to the property but this can only be exercise when the court has given the mortgagee the power of sale. Under this arrangement, whatever is proceeds realized by the receiver will be used to offset the loan.

4.1.2.3.4 Foreclosure

Foreclosure as a method of realizing a mortgage can be defined as the destruction of the mortgagor right of redemption[44]. Also, it refers to collection of debt (usually mortgage) by seizing and selling the debtor's property or security[45].

Under this method, an application for foreclosure must be granted by court, and when granted the mortgagee becomes the absolute owner of the property but this practice is not popular amongst bank.

---

[42] Hornby A. S. *Oxford Advanced Learners Dictionary*. Oxford University Press. USA 7th Edition, 2006. P.1470

[43] Hornby A. S. *Oxford Advanced Learners Dictionary*. Oxford University Press. USA 7th Edition, 2006. P.1214

[44] Afolabi, Layi .*Law and Practice of Banking*. Heinemann Educational books Nig. Ibadan 1999. P 316

[45] Hartzell, D. Dictionary of Management. Ogun. Melrose Books and Publishing, 2011. P.153

Though, such application can only be granted after when the mortgagor is unable to do the needful to reclaim its property after a reasonable time.

4.1.2.3.5 Enter Into Possession

The banks can enter into possession of the landed property considering the fact that it has a security interest in the title of the said property. Under this method, the bank can appoint a manager to collects rents on the property which is to be used to service the loan until full payment. At the end the bank is expected to account for the receipt of the payments during the periods it remains in possession.

4.1.2.3.6 Sale

Under this method, the bank has an automatic right to sell the property considering the fact that it was made under deed. This is further supported by Section 123 of the Property and Conveyance law of 1956 which stipulates that

" *a mortgagee where the mortgage is made by deed shall by virtue of this law, have the following powers to the extent as if they had been in terms conferred by the mortgage deed, but no further namely; a power, when the mortgage money has become due, to sell or to concur with any other person in selling the mortgage property.*

Though, before selling such a property there are certain conditions which must be fulfilled as provided in Section 125 of the same law which is summarized as thus; *notices requiring payment must be served for 3months, interest under the mortgage must be in arrears and unpaid for 2 months and they exist some breach of the provision in the mortgage deed.*

Upon the sale of the property, the proceeds will be credited to the loan account so as to offset the debit balance and the remaining balance if any will be left for the customer.

4.2 Debenture as a Security

A debenture is an instrument issued under a common seal of the company acknowledging its debt to the holder under the terms and conditions specified in the instruments[46]. Similarly, debenture can also be defined as a document issued by a company as evidence of its corporate indebtedness[47].

From the definitions presented, we can deduce that debentures are normally issued by a company which is usually under seal stating out certain terms and conditions of the debt. However, in Nigeria the creation of debentures by a company is empowered by the CAMA act of 1990, section 166 (1) which states that

" *a company may borrow for the purpose of its business or objective and may mortgage or charge its undertaking, property and uncalled capital or any part there off issue debenture, debenture stock and over securities whether outright or as security for any debt, liability or obligation of the company or any third party".*

Debentures issued by a company can be either convertible, Non-Convertible and partly convertible debentures, these are debentures that can be easily converted into shares depending on the terms of issue with regards to price, the time of conversion. Non-Convertible debentures are debentures that cannot be converted into shares while partly convertible debentures are hybrid debenture that has features of convertible and non convertible options.

In addition, debenture can be viewed from 2 types depending upon the availability or non availability of security for their repayment which is either Secured or non- secured debenture. Secured debentures are debentures created with charge over security while non-secured debentures which is also called naked debenture are created without charge to security.

However, under the secured form of debentures, different types of debentures can be created/charge over the company's asset.

4.2.1 Types of Charge

Basically there are three (3) types of charge over a company's asset which is as follows

[46] Hartzell, D. Dictionary of Management. Ogun. Melrose Books and Publishing, 2011. P.99

[47] Onyiriuba Leo . *Analysing and Managing Risk of Bank Lending*. NFS Data Bureau Ltd. Lagos Second Edition. 2008. P. 381

i. Floating charge (Floating debenture)

ii. Fixed Charge (Mortgage debenture)

iii. All Asset debentures

4.2.1.1 Floating Charge

Floating charge refers to an equitable charge over the whole or a specific part of the company's undertaking and asset including cash and uncalled capital of the company both present and future.[48] This includes raw material, stock, debt, work in progress etc. this type of charge exclude the company's fixed asset.

However, this form of charge crystallizes when the company goes into liquidation; court appoints a receiver or manager of such asset on the application of the holder or enters into possession[49].

4.2.1.1.1 Advantages of Floating Charge

i. The process, cost involved in creation of this form of charge is very simple and cost effective compared to a fixed charge.

ii. During liquidation, floating charge are given priority over unsecured creditors.

iii. The fact that it involves charge over the floating asset of a company both the present and future, such security will be appreciable and safer if the company grows.

4.2.1.1.2 Disadvantages of Floating Charge

i. There exists the problem of valuation of such asset as there are no specific standards in measuring such asset just as the case of life insurance where there exist an acceptable standard for obtaining the surrender value.

ii. The condition or value of such asset at the point of default might be worthless to offset the facility amount thus, makes realization difficult.

---

[48] CAMA Act (1990). Section 178(1)
[49] CAMA Act (1990). 178(1)a-c

iii. Creation of floating charge is also a problem because section 179 of CAMA Act 1990 has given priority of fixed charge over floating charge. The case of Wilson Vs Kellard (1910)[50] can also attest to this fact.

iv. There also exists a problem of priority of other creditors apart from the fixed charge. Amongst which are liquidation expenses, preferential claims and judgment creditors.

v. In Nigeria, Section 498 of the CAMA act also constitute a major disadvantage to the creation of floating charge on the undertaking or property of the company created within 3months of the commencement of winding up shall, unless proved that the company immediately after the creation of the charge was solvent, be invalid except to the creation of and in consideration.

4.2.1.2 Fixed Charge

Fixed charge is a mortgage on specific asset which deprives the company of the right to deal with such asset in any manner prejudice to the rights of the debenture holder[51]. This type of charge is created as a form of legal mortgage and once created the company cannot deal or dispose of the asset without the bank prior approval. Such asset involves land, building plants etc.

Fixed charge by its nature has a priority over the floating charge once created but it is better effective if the bank is not aware of any prior charge over such asset.

4.2.1.2.1 Advantages of Fixed Charge

i. Fixed charge has a priority advantage over floating charge as supported in section 179 of the CAMA act of 1990 " *A fixed charge on any property shall have priority over a floating charge affecting that property unless… ….*

ii. The bank has the power or right to appoint an official receiver to dispose off the asset of the company in times of liquidation.

---

[50]L.J.580.(79)

[51] Robert Igben, *Financial Accounting made Simple*. Lagos. Roi Publishers.Vol. 1. 3rd Edition. P.398

iii. The fact that it is attached to specific asset that are fixed in nature which are not easily movable, it is difficult for the debtor to abscond with such security.

iv. Most of the asset that are attached to fixed charge has a relatively stable price/value hence realization is not a problem.

4.2.1.2.2 Disadvantages of Fixed Charge

i. The process, cost involved in creating a fixed charge over an asset of a company is time consuming and expensive in nature.

ii. Depreciation may affect the asset which will invariably has effect on its value, thus posing a danger in times of realization

iii. The fact the a fixed charge is attached to specific asset of the company, the same asset will be used to offset the facility in case of default and if the value of such asset declines due to one reason or the other, the bank will be considered as an unsecured creditor on the value of the outstanding sum.

4.2.1.3 All Asset Debentures

This involves a charge on both the floating and fixed asset of the company. This type of charge is stronger than a floating charge but weaker than a fixed charge because no specific asset is attached to it[52], no power to appoint a receiver or sell the asset without court permission.

4.2.2 Major Clauses Considered In a Debenture

There are certain clauses that exist in a debenture which is binding upon the debtors and creditors. Amongst such clauses are as follows[53]:-

[52] Afolabi, Layi .*Law and Practice of Banking*. Heinemann Educational books Nig. Ibadan 1999. P 279-281
[53] Spring Bank plc Standard Form on Debenture

i. **Continuing Security:-**This clause is very important in a debenture as it is usually included to prevent the application of the rule in Clayton case and also to make the security valid for all future debt even if the original debt has been paid.

ii. **Overdraft repayable on demand:-** this implies that the facility amount is payable on demand by the lender. This empowers the lender to request for the repayment upon expiry or when there is a breach in its terms and conditions.

iii. **Undertaken to Keep asset insured and good maintenance:-** This clause ensures that the so called pledge asset be insured by a reputable insurance company which the lenders interest be noted as first loss payee. One advantage of this clause is to check the way and manner by which the borrower behaves with the asset pledge.

iv. **Right to appoint a Receiver:-**This clause gives the lender the right to appoint a receiver in case of default in order to realize its exposure.

v. **Undertaken not to create another charge:-** This clause serves as a form of Negative pledge. It give the lender the sole charge over the company's asset despite the fact that such company can still create a further charge depending on the margins of the value of the asset.

vi. **Undertakings to provide details of the company's asset and liabilities and audited accounts:-** this clause put the borrower on alert that its activities is been monitored via such reports. The report can be rendered monthly, quarterly, half yearly etc depending upon the terms they agreed.

4.2.3 Documentary Requirements

The following are the documentary requirements needed by both a lender and borrower in creating debentures.[54] Amongst which are:-

i. Title documents for the fixed asset.

ii. Memorandum and Article of association (MEMART) of the company

[54] Enterprise Bank Limited, Credit Policy Manual, Feb,2012

iii. A copy of certificate of incorporation of the company

iv. 3 year of financial report of the company for an evaluation of the book value of the asset.

v. Valuation report of the company asset.

vi. Board resolution authorizing the borrowing and creation of the debentures.

vii. Evidence of PAYE of the company and that of at least 2 directors of the company.

viii. Current TCC of the company and those of at least 2 directors of the company.

ix. Insurance policy of such asset where the bank interest is noted as First loss payee.

x. Duly executed debenture deed by the company (2 directors or one director and the company secretary.

4.2.4 Perfection of a Debenture

Upon fulfilling the documentary requirements, the following a process should be followed and executed for a debenture to be perfected.

i. Registration of Debenture deed as required by section 197 of the CAMA act of 1990; that is the registration must be done within 90 days after the date of creation of the deed at Corporate Affairs commission (CAC) and upon such a Certificate of registration will be issued as evidence.

ii. Stamping of the Deed: Registration and stamping of the deed are two different things. The stamping is a pre-requisite for its registration both at the land registry in case of landed properties and at Corporate Affairs commission (CAC).

4.2.5 Determination of a Debenture

A debenture is determined upon the occurrence of the following:[55]-

i. If the company goes into liquidation.

[55] CAMA Act (1990). Section 208(1)

ii. Where the company also fails to service its debt.

iii. There exist breaches in the terms and condition on the debenture deed.

iv. If the court appoints a receiver or manager.

v. Where the company ceases to carry on its business

4.2.6 Realization of a Debenture

The following are the methods or remedies available to a lender in case of any default by the borrower[56].

i. Sue for the debt

ii. Appointment of an official receiver

iii. Apply for foreclosure

iv. Invoke the power of sale of the asset

v. Commence winding up procedure by presenting a petition against the company on the grounds of its inability to meet its obligation as at when due.

4.3 Stocks or Shares as a Security

A share may be described as the legal interest of a shareholder in the authorized and issued capital of a company measured by a sum of money for the purpose of liability in the first place and of participation in the second place[57]. It can also be defined as a unit of or reckoning investors interest in the contributed capital of a company[58].

Shares of a company can be broadly categorized as follows; the ordinary and preference shares[59]. The ordinary shares are the legal owners of the company. They are entitled to dividend which is not fixed as in the case of a preference shares. Ordinary shares are considered a permanent source of capital to a company.

---

[56] Afolabi, Layi .*Law and Practice of Banking.* Heinemann Educational books Nig. Ibadan 1999. P 279-281; Onyiriuba Leo . *Analysing and Managing Risk of Bank Lending.* NFS Data Bureau Ltd. Lagos Second Edition. 2008 and CAMA Act (1990). Section 209.

[57] CAMA Act of 1990. Part V. P.32

[58] Hartzell, D. Dictionary of Management. Ogun. Melrose Books and Publishing, 2011. P.343

The ordinary share of a company can be subdivided into Authorized share capital, issue share capital, subscribe share capital and paid up share capital. The preference share is a type of share that its holders are entitle to a fixed dividend from the company be it whether profit are made or not and also they are given preferential treatment as the name implies over the ordinary share holders in all ramification such as payment of dividend, liquidation etc. preferential share is mostly considered to be an hybrid security because it has both features of ordinary shares and debentures. Preferential shares can be cumulative or non cumulative.

Shares of a company can be used or pledge a security for bank lending by submitting its relevant document like share certificate but the type of company shares matters because companies that are not quoted on the list of stock exchange are not advisable as there exist so many restrictions and difficulties in its realization. A company is said to be quoted on the list of stock exchange are often refers to as public limited liability company (PLC) which is normally written at the end of the company name.

However, for a non listed company share; it poses some problem in terms of accepting it as a security

i. There exists problem a problem of determining the market value of such share as there exist no organized market.

ii. Realization is also considered as a big problem associated in such type of shares.

iii. The CAMA act of 1990 also constitute a problem as stated in section 22 where it defines a private company as one which is stated in its memo to be a private company.

a. Every private company shall by its article restrict the transfers of its shares.

b. The total number of members shall not exceed 50 not including persons who are bonafide in the employment of the company.

c. Prohibits any invitation to the public to subscribe for its shares or debentures.

---

[59] Robert Igben, *Financial Accounting made Simple*. Lagos. Roi Publishers.Vol. 1. 3rd Edition. P.376

Notwithstanding of company that is quoted has also some benefits over non quoted any in the following areas amongst which are, position of transfer of shares, reduction in cost of capital, Better pricing of shares, enhance credit rating of such any tendency of takeover and merges, enhance the profile of such company

Despite, the numerous advantage of a company on the floor of a stock exchange it has some of its shortcomings such as high cost of floatation, dilution of ownership and control, Exposure to Public Scrutiny and possible takeover.

4.3.1 Factors to be Considered When Accepting Shares or Stock

Before considering other factors, it is very pertinent that it is prohibited for a bank to accepts its own shares as a security as stated in section 20(1b) of the BOFID which states that;

A bank shall not, without the prior approval in writing of the bank grant any advances, loans or credit facilities against the security of its own shares or any unsecured advances, loans or credit facilities unless authorised in accordance with the banks rules and regulations and where any such rules and regulations require adequate security, such security shall be provided or as the case may require, deposited with the bank".

Other factors also to consider are as follows;

i. Type of Share:

Under this factor, certain questions are considered whether it is an ordinary shares or preference share or whether it is quoted or not. But the former is very important because accepting shares that is not quoted on the floor of the stock exchange is very difficult to realize upon default and other related problems associated with such type of shares has been earlier discussed.

ii. Valuation

Valuation is considered an important aspect in every form of security. The valuation procedure involves in shares and stock depends on the current market price of such shares which is usually published on the daily quotation list. But most at times it is preferable to accept a confirmed current stock position from Central Security Clearing System.

iii. Margin

Margin of the value of the stock and the loan amount should be taken into consideration. Not because the market position of such shares is equivalent to the loan amount then such security is suitable. There is need for a margin so as to take care of any unforeseen circumstances surrounding the shares as the value of the shares is grossly determined by the forces of demand and supply. Thus its value is subject to fluctuations.

However, most banks has different standards or bench mark in accepting shares as some may set 120% which implies that the value of the shares should be at least 120% of the facility amount.

iv. Type of Mortgage

This factor has to do with the type of mortgage to be created on such shares whether an equitable or legal mortgage. But the later is preferable to the banks because the title of the share is assigned to the bank. Details of the type of mortgage will be explained later in subsequent sub headings.

4.3.2 Creation of Mortgage on Shares

The methods of creating mortgage over shares or stocks are as follows:-

i. Equitable mortgage

ii. Legal Mortgage

iii. Operation of the law. i.e causing a court of law to make a charge order on shares or stock

4.3.2.1 Equitable Mortgage over Shares

The equitable mortgage involves the simple deposit of share certificate with the bank as the title on such shares is not transfer to the lender. Under the equitable mortgage, the charge is created in two (2) ways[60]:

i. Simple deposit of Share Certificate with or without executing the Memorandum of deposit.

---

[60] Afolabi, Layi .*Law and Practice of Banking*. Heinemann Educational books Nig. Ibadan 1999. P 279-281

ii. Simple deposit of Share certificate with executing the memorandum of deposit and execution of a blank share transfer form .

From the charge mentioned, the second type is the best because in this form of mortgage, executing the memorandum of deposit has completely waive the borrower claims in the future that his intention is safe deposit and the blank share transfer form has automatically given the bank the power of sale upon default.

The memorandum of deposit contains viable clause that has committed the customer. Amongst such clause are

i. All advances are payable on demand

ii. Express undertaking by the customer to transfer the equitable to legal if required by the bank.

iii. Affirmation that the bank is entitle to all benefits accruing to the share

iv. Continuing security clause (to avoid the operation of the Clayton case against the bank)

4.3.2.1.1 Documentary Requirements

Below are the documents needed for creating charges over shares[61]:-

i. Original Share certificate

ii. Duly executed memorandum of deposit of shares

iii. Duly executed share transfer form

iv. An undated letter of consent from the borrower to sell the shares.

4.3.2.1.2 Procedures for Creating Equitable Charge over Shares

Under the equitable charge the sole objective of the bank is to create a lien on the pledge shares[62]. The following are the procedures

[61] Enterprise Bank Limited, Credit Policy Manual, Feb,2012

i. The borrower will make available to the bank the stock position slip issued by CSCS.

ii. The bank will confirm the slip from CSCS

iii. The joint memorandum will be executed by both parties requesting CSCS to place lien on the stated shareholding.

iv. The customer signs an undated letter authorizing the bank to sell the shares upon default.

v. The Customer executes the dividend mandate and lodge with the registrar.

vi. Register the memo with the commissioner for stamp duties or High court.

vii. The parties will be invited by CSCS to confirm the lien agreement.

viii. Upon receipt of the memo, the share holding will be moved to the CSCS reserved lien account with the interest of the lender noted.

ix. CSCS will advise the bank confirming the lien placement on the shares.

However, in case of default the following steps are to be followed

i. The bank will inform the borrower of his default, notice to also exercise the option to sell the shares.

ii. The lender will officially write the CSCS of the default thereby advising CSCS to remove lien to enable sale effected.

iii. The bank can now invoke the undated letter authorizing the sale of shares via it stock broking firm.

iv. If CSCS is satisfied, they will comply.

---

[62] Onyiriuba Leo . *Analysing and Managing Risk of Bank Lending.* NFS Data Bureau Ltd. Lagos Second Edition. 2008.P385; John E. I . "Practice of Banking" CIBN *Exam Distance Learning Pack.* PE III.. Accountancy Training and Publication Ltd. Lagos 2011. Pp. 125-147

4.3.2.1.3 Advantages of Equitable Mortgage over Shares

i. The process, time and cost involved in creating equitable charge over shares is less expensive compared to legal mortgage.

ii. The issues of director share qualification (i.e. if the company makes the director shareholding compulsory) do not affect this type of mortgage.

iii. The bank can also apply to court for an order of sale in case of default.

iv. The bank can also sue on the debt

4.3.2.1.4 Disadvantages of Equitable Mortgage over Shares

i. Legal mortgage over shares takes priority over equitable mortgage once created in good faith and without notice of an existing charge.

ii. Realization is sometimes difficult as the bank does not have title over the shares and also court assistance is usually required.

iii. The borrower can also outsmart the bank by obtaining a new certificate under indemnity and transferring same to another bank.

4.3.3 Legal Mortgage over Shares

This has to do with the conveyance of the legal interest in shares as security for a debt or for a discharge of an obligation. Thus, the title of the shares is to been transferred to the bank and upon payment of the facility amount, the bank will then reassign the interest back to the borrower.

Under this arrangement, the bank has the following rights such as right to dividends, right to bonus share, right to vote at company's' meeting and right to transfer shares. This form of mortgage is the best form of creating charge over shares as the banks position in all aspect is safe.

4.3.3.1 Procedure for Creating Legal Mortgage over Shares

The procedure for creating legal mortgage is as follows:-

i. The borrower will make available to the bank the stock position slip issued by CSCS.

ii. The bank will confirm the slip from CSCS

iii. Share transfer form will be duly signed by the customer

iv. CSCS will send information on the transfer of the shareholding.

v. The registrar will update the register of the shareholder and a new share certificate will be issued in favour of the bank.

vi. Upon issuance of a new certificate, the mortgage has been perfected, thus all bonuses, dividend will be issued to the bank for onward credit to the borrowers account.

4.3.3.2 Advantages of Legal Mortgage over Shares

The advantages of legal mortgage are as follows;

i. It has a priority over equitable mortgage.

ii. It gives the bank a perfect title to the shares.

iii. Court assistance is not required during realization

iv. Dividend, bonuses, right issues are routed through the bank to the customer, thus has a good impact on the value of the shares.

4.3.3.3 Disadvantages of Legal Mortgage over Shares

The disadvantages of the form of charge are as follows:

i. The process or formalities involved in creating the legal mortgage is time consuming and tedious.

ii. The cost of creating the legal mortgage is expensive compared to equitable mortgage.

iii. Legal Mortgage cannot be created over shares that directors share qualification is compulsory.

iv. There exists a tendency of forged share transfer as in the case of Sheffield Corporation Vs Barclay bank (1905)[63].

v. Legal mortgage cannot be charge on shares when they are not fully paid-up.

4.4 *Life Insurance Policy as a Security*

A Life insurance (or assurance) policy is a contract whereby in return for a lump sum or regular payment, the company provides an agreed sum to the policy holder's estate in the event of death before sum agreed date or the policy holder upon survival to this date[64].

Life assurance can also be defined as a contract whereby the insurer in consideration of a premium paid by the assured undertakes to pay in the event of death of a named person certain sum of money to a person named by the assured[65]. From the definition above, we can deduce that the parties involved in a life insurance policy are Insurer, assured and beneficiary.

The operations of insurance contract in whatever form or class is based on the doctrine of *Uberrimae Fidae*- the utmost good faith. This implies that it is duty bond on parties to disclose all material facts involved in the contract and failure to do such amount to fraud which the aggrieved party can cancel or repudiate the contract.

In addition, the concept of insurable interest cannot be over emphasized when ever insurance is mentioned. This has to do with whether the beneficiary has an insurance interest in the life of the assured eg Employer and Employee etc because in absence of it such a contract is null and void, unenforceable as provided in the British Life Assurance Act of 1774. So also the principle of indemnity and subrogation cannot be ruled out as it also constitutes the basic principles underlying an insurance contract.

---

[63] A.C.392

[64] Black . J (2002). *Oxford Dictionary of Economics*. USA. Oxford University press. P.269
[65] Onyiriuba Leo . *Analysing and Managing Risk of Bank Lending*. NFS Data Bureau Ltd. Lagos Second Edition. 2008.P385

However the *modus operandi* of insurance is within the confined of the ordinary law of contract which implies that the offer and acceptance is applicable which must be unconditional. Life assurance policy is basically classified into two[66]; Whole Life assurance Policy and Endowment policy.

i. Whole Life Policy

The whole life policy is a form of life assurance policy which is payable on the death of the assured. This form of policy is only effective upon the death of the assured which is not a good form of security due to the uncertainty as regards the death of the assured.

ii. Endowment Policy

This form of policy is payable upon the maturity or death of the assured. This policy has strike a balance because whichever incidence that occur (death or maturity) the policy is effectively determined. This is considered as a good security for banks.

Having discussed the types of insurance policy that exist, it is pertinent to consider some of the factors banks should consider before accepting it as a form of security without any exposure.

4.4.1 Critical Factors to be considered when accepting Insurance Policy

There are certain critical success factors to be taken into consideration when accepting insurance as a security for bank lending[67] because failure to abide by such factors will create loopholes on the security which at the end will make such security unrealizable. Amongst such factors are:-

i. Insurance Company

---

[66] John E. I . "Practice of Banking" CIBN Exam Distance Learning Pack. PE III.. Accountancy Training and Publication Ltd. Lagos 2011. Pp. 125-147;

[67] John E. I . "Practice of Banking" CIBN *Exam Distance Learning Pack.* PE III.. Accountancy Training and Publication Ltd. Lagos 2011. Pp. 125-147; Afolabi, Layi .*Law and Practice of Banking.* Heinemann Educational books Nig. Ibadan 1999. P 279-281

The bank is to ensure that the insurer of the company is duly registered with the Director of Insurance as required by Section 4 of the insurance Decree No. 1, 1997 and also the history of the insurer payment of claims also should be factor in accessing the company.

ii. Type of Insurance Policy

The type of insurance policy is very key to be taken into consideration as they exist certain type of insurance policy that cannot be assigned and its maturity period might be uncertain just as the case of whole life insurance policy where it is only payable upon the death of the assured.

iii. Surrender Value

This represents the amount of money one obtains from terminating life insurance policy before its maturity. It is the pay for pre-mature termination of the insurance policy. The value of the surrender value is very certain as it has a standard for valuation. Surrender value is dependent on the sum insured, premium, duration of the policy, type of policy etc.

However, in accepting insurance policy as a form of security against lending, it is advisable that the lender should not lend above the surrender value as it is preferable to ensure that there is a margin between the facility amount and the surrender value. Though, banks have different benchmark for determining such margin.

iv. Insurable Interest

This factor is very important as the bank is to ensure that the beneficiary of the policy has an insurable interest in the policy as failure of such interest render it null and void as stipulated in Section 1 of the British life Assurance Act of 1774. By insurable interest we refer to as the financial interest in a person, organization, services or goods for which there is a possibility of financial loss that can be actually determined and rated and which warrants the purchase of production[68] . For instance a creditor has an insurable interest in the life of a debtor while in the case of a life assurance the assured has an insurable interest in his own life.

v. Age of the Assured

[68] Hartzell, D. Dictionary of Management. Ogun. Melrose Books and Publishing, 2011. P.199

The age of the assured is also very important in the life assurance policy as it is considered amongst the variable in the calculation of the premium. However, if the age of the assured is not noted, it is important to request for a declaration of age or birth certificate in order to authenticate the information because if the age is understated it will have a great effect on the risk and premium and when discovered could lead to termination of such contract as the basis of insurance is *Uberimae Fidae*- (Utmost good faith) which implies that all material facts should be disclosed by contracting parties.

vi. Restriction

The lender is to ensure that terms and conditions of the policy is well digested so as not to put the bank to danger because failure to abide by such restriction or clauses could render the security null and void. Amongst such clauses are assignment clauses (Whether or not such policy can be assigned to another), occupational clauses (preventing the assured from certain occupation), and travelling clauses (Preventing the assured from travelling without approval from the insurance company).

vii. Prior Assignment

This is also very important that the lender should also ensure that such policy is not previously assigned to another bank and if such is previously charge, the discharge from such prior charge should be submitted along side with the policy. In addition if there exist a charge on the policy then the bank should be able to know the extent of the exposure of the first charge via the surrender value of the policy so as to know whether or not it can have a second charge over the same policy when compared with the facility amount

However, the type of charge matters because if the first charge is an equitable charge and the second charge is a legal charge created without knowledge of the first charge, the second charge automatically gains priority over the first charge.

viii. Exclusion

It is kind that banks should be mindful of the exclusion clauses in a life assurance policy. For instance, some policy will not be paid if the death is caused by situation like war, ex-judicial death sentenced of the assured, suicide etc.

4.4.2 Assignment of Insurance Policy

Insurance policy can be assigned to bank as a security against loans and advances in the following ways:-

4.4.2.1 Equitable Assignment

This has to do with the simple deposit of original life policy with or without execution of memorandum of deposit. Details of such charge have already been discussed earlier.

4.4.2.2 Legal Assignment

This is in fact the best method of assignment banks should adopt as it has to do with assigning the interest of the policy to the bank pending the repayment before such will be reassigned back to the borrower. This is usually done by the borrower executing the deed of assignment which must be stamped and registered and notice sent to the insurance company that is when it is said to be duly perfected. Details of such charge have already been discussed earlier.

However, under both forms of assignment second charge or sub-mortgage can also be created over the life policy.

4.4.3 Documentary Requirements

The documents required for the creation of a charge over the life assurance policy are as follows:-

i. Original copy of the life policy

ii. Receipt of the last premium paid

iii. Copy of discharge letter if policy has been previously charge.

iv. Copy of the surrender value from the insurance company

v. Duly executed deed of assignment form

vi. Notice of assignment and acknowledge copy from the insurance company

vii. Letter of standing order payment of the insurance premium.

4.4.4 Realization of an Insurance Policy

The option available for the realization of the insurance policy can be summed as SOS- which literally refers to urgent request for help[69] but in this context it refers to as S- Surrender the policy, O- Obtain Loan, S- Sell the policy.

i. Surrender the Policy

This is considered as the best option for realizing insurance policy upon default by the borrower on its terms and condition. Life assurance can be said to be redeemable upon either maturity or death of the assured or whichever comes first.

Under this method of realizing such security the bank liaise with the insurer or insurance company and complete the claims forms and other documents such as assignment forms, the original policy, and death certificate- if the assured is dead. And upon completion the surrender value or the capital sum of the policy will be paid directly to the bank.

ii. Obtaining Loan

This refers to a situation where by the insurance company will grant a loan to a certain percentage of the surrender value to the bank so as to offset the outstanding debt. This method is better suitable if the outstanding debt is very less than the surrender value of the policy and the policy is yet to mature.

iii. Selling the Policy

Under the deed of legal assignment the bank the power to sell the security is automatic as it does not require court assistance as in the case of equitable assignment. In this case the bank can sell the policy to buyers or financial institution that specializes in the buying of insurance policy. Under this method, there exists the fact there exist a tendency of selling above or below the surrender value.

4.4.5 Advantages of Life Policy

Life assurance policy as some advantages which are as follows:

[69] Hornby A. S. *Oxford Advanced Learners Dictionary*. Oxford University Press. USA 7th Edition, 2006. P.1407

i. Investigation of title to the policy is very simple to carry out.

ii. The cost of assignment is relatively low when compared to legal mortgage for landed properties.

iii. The value of the surrender value increases when premium are continued to be paid as at when due.

iv. Establishing the value of the policy is very easy as there exists certain standard used in valuation.

v. Realization of such security is very simple.

4.4.6 Disadvantages of Life Policy

The disadvantages of the policy are as follows:-

i. Realization of such policy depends on the reputation of the insurance company in terms of claims settlement.

ii. The policy is considered void, if the beneficiary has no insurable interest in the life of the assured.

iii. The policy if newly taken will have no surrender value, thus accepting such will jeopardize the security as realising will be problems.

iv. Failure to pay the premium as at when due can repudiate the policy.

v. If the policy is taken by more than one person it might be difficult to join all parties.

vi. It operates on the principle of *uberimae fidae* as all necessary material information will be disclosed by parties, failure to observe such invalidate the contact.

4.5 Guarantee as a Security

Guarantee, according refers to as a person who promises that if a second person fails to fulfill some obligation then he will fulfill it or pay up to a specified limit to compensate for any loss caused by the second person failure[70].

[70] Hartzell, D. Dictionary of Management. Ogun. Melrose Books and Publishing, 2011. P.172

Similarly, it can also be defined as a tripartite relationship where by a person called the guarantor undertakes which usually in written to indemnify the bank against any loss arising from the default of the other party called the principal debtor[71].

From the definitions', we can deduce that there exist three (3) parties in guarantee which is Guarantor, bank and debtor. It is therefore pertinent to state that the liability of the guarantor is both dependent and a secondary type. It is dependent or primary if for any reason the contract between the debtor and creditor is invalid and a secondary if the debtor defaults. Most often, a contract of a guarantee is miss-understood to mean a contract of indemnity.

A contact of indemnity is an arrangement whereby one person agree to make good any loss suffered by a party to a contract to which himself is a stranger[72]. Below are some of the differences that exist between a contract of Guarantee and a contract of indemnity.

i. In a contract of guarantee, there exist 3 parties (Guarantor, Bank and Debtor) while in a case of indemnity there exist only two (2) parties.

ii. A guarantee is statutorily required to be in writing (Section 4 of the Statute of Fraud of 1774) where as indemnity is not required.

iii. A contract of indemnity is a contract of *uberimae Fadei*- Utmost good faith but the contract of indemnity is not.

iv. The liability that exist in a contract of Guarantee are two (2); primary and secondary liability but in the case of indemnity there exist only a primary liability.

Guarantee as security against lending are of two (2) types namely[73]:-

i. Personal Guarantee

ii. Corporate Guarantee.

4.5.1 Personal Guarantee

[71] Onyiriuba Leo . *Analysing and Managing Risk of Bank Lending*. NFS Data Bureau Ltd. Lagos Second Edition. 2008.P386
[72] Hartzell, D. Dictionary of Management. Ogun. Melrose Books and Publishing, 2011. P.189
[73] Onyiriuba Leo . *Analysing and Managing Risk of Bank Lending*. NFS Data Bureau Ltd. Lagos Second Edition. 2008.P387

This type of guarantee is mostly required when banks are lending to individuals or companies. However, the case of a company is more pronounced because the directors are usually required to guarantee their company in view of the fact of the concept of legal entity of a company. This will make it easy to figure out who will be held responsible for the breach of the terms and conditions of the loan.

Amongst documents required for this type of guarantee are

i. Duly dated executed personal guarantee form

ii. Notarized statement of Net worth of the guarantor and asset duly inspected.

iii. A Passport Photograph of the guarantor

iv. A valid means of Identification Card of the Guarantor.

However, in accepting guarantee, the credit worthiness of the guarantor should be establish, status inquiry, background checks, need to be carried out to ensure that such person is reliable and worthy to be a guarantor. The following cannot stand as a guarantor, Minor, Unsound mind person, Person under influence, Debtor guarantee itself, Person once declared as bankrupt, partnership-one party cannot, Limited Liability Company.

4.5.2 Corporate Guarantee

This is a type of guarantee usually issued by company on behalf or an individual or another company. This is mostly issued by company on behalf of its subsidiaries or sister company recommending their credit worthiness and capacity. Corporate guarantee are normally issued by company duly signed by 2 directors or a director and the company secretary which is duly stamped by the company seal.

In addition, there exist basic things that bank should check before accepting a corporate guarantee from a company. Amongst such are

i. Confirm authenticity of the company whether it is duly registered with Corporate Affairs Commission (CAC) or not.

ii. The Company's MEMART- whether its MEMARTs empowers it to issue such guarantee because non failure leads to ultra virus which is consider as Null and Void.

iii. Net worth of the company- Asset and Liabilities

iv. Board resolution authorizing the guarantee

v. Check the concept of commercial justification for issuing such guarantee- that is to ensure that the company asset are not applied without without corresponding benefit to the company and interest directors in Section 270 of the CAMA act, 1990.

" it shall not be lawful for a company to make a loan to any person who is a director or a director of its holding or to enter into any guarantee or provide security in connection with a loan made to such person".

4.5.3 Advantages of a Guarantee

The advantages of a guarantee are as follows:

i. The formalities involved in guarantee are very simple.

ii. The cost involved in collecting guarantee is less expensive compared to other forms of security.

iii. It does not involved investigation of title.

iv. It ensures greater commitment on the part of the borrower and its guarantor.

v. The value of such security is relatively stable because the more as the guarantor progress it directly affects its net worth.

4.5.4 Disadvantages of a Guarantee

The disadvantages of a guarantee are as follows:-

i. There exists a problem of realization resulting to protracted court action or order.

ii. There exist problem such as undue influences, misrepresentation etc which most a times guarantor rely upon to defend or outsmart banks.

iii. Court assistance is normally required to realize as these involved cost which is expensive.

iv. Most a times the death of the guarantor possesses a lot of problem to the security.

v. There exist situations where by the net worth of the guarantors declines due to one reason or another and this may affect the facility upon realization.

4.5.5 Determination of a Guarantee

Guarantee can be determine by various ways or circumstances as this has to do with calling in the guarantor. A guarantee can be determined as follows:-

i. Upon Demand by the Bank

A Guarantee is determined when the bank demand payment of the debt from the guarantor. Such step is invoke after when the principal debtor has defaulted on the loans terms and conditions and has been asked to repay the loan or when the bank decide to recall the facility.

ii. Repayment by the Guarantor

A guarantee can also be said to be discharge if the guarantor willingly paid the limit of his guarantee to the bank.

iii. Demand by the Guarantor

This can also be seen as a way in which the guarantee can be determined because a guarantor might decide to give notice to the bank that he is no longer acting as a surety to the principal debtor and by such notice the bank is expected to discharge him/her.

iv. Bankruptcy of Guarantor or Debtor

By bankruptcy, we refer to a situation in which debtors are not only insolvent (unable to pay debts as and when they become due) but have made it clear that they are unable to do so and do not expect to pay their debt in full[74].

When the principal debtor is been declared bankrupt and the bank has receive such notice, the guarantor will be call in most a times simultaneously while trying to recover the debt from the trustee or personal representative. Likewise, if a guarantor is declared bankrupt the guarantee will be called in so as to recover the guarantee limit from trustee or personal representative or executors.

v. Mental Incapacity of the Guarantor or Debtor

This refers to a situation whereby the guarantor or principal debtor loses his or her legal capacity; this means the ability to incur legal liability or to acquire legal rights. Whenever such events occurs, the guarantee is immediately determined as it is advisable for the bank to formally make claim of the debt from the receiver, trustee but it is pertinent to note that the guarantee at a point of his or her loses or declared mental incapacitated but any future debt after such period he or she cannot be held liable.

In a similar vein, if a principal debtor is declared mental incapacitated, the guarantee is immediately called in by the bank while simultaneously trying to ensure that the outstanding debt are recovered from the receiver.

vi. Death of the Guarantor or Debtor

Upon the receipt of notice of death of a guarantor the guarantee is immediately called in so that the limit of the guarantee can be recovered and by this the bank can formally notify the trustee or personal representative etc on the outstanding debt to ensure full recovery in order to avoid the principal debtor takes undue advantage. Likewise, if it's the death of the principal debtor the bank will invite the surety on how he or she can pay off his limit of the guarantee and also the bank can also apply to the personal representative in order to recover the outstanding debt.

vii. Change in Status of the Debtor

---

[74] Hartzell, D. Dictionary of Management. Ogun. Melrose Books and Publishing, 2011. P.30

If there is a notice of change of status of the principal debtor may be from either individual to a company or firm to company etc in the nutshell, a change of its legal status, the guarantee is immediately determined but changes internally cannot determined the guarantee.

4.6 Goods as a Security

Good as a concept has different definition but however we shall consider few amongst them. Goods refer to as an economic asset taking a tangible physical form[75].

Goods includes, unless the context or subject matter otherwise requires, all chattels personal other than things in action and money[76]. Thus the term cover varying object such as clothes, shoes, motor car, machinery, books, furniture and growing crops. Goods can be existing goods, future goods, unascertained goods or Specific or ascertain goods[77].Goods are highly considered as a form of security against lending by banks. In such a case banks do not physically take possession of the goods but goes after the title to the goods.

In a bid to adequately explore the opportunity of using goods as a form of security, products such as Import and Export finance facility, Letter of credit etc were developed to suite or satisfy the needs of these customers. Under such arrangement the bank can finance part of the request which implies that the customer has to provide equity of either 20% or 30% even above depending on the banks credit policy.

Under such security arrangement, there exist certain documents which give banks title to the goods. Amongst such are bills of lading, delivery warrants or order, warehouse receipt or certificate. Furthermore, in accepting goods are a form of security there are certain factors to be considered by banks.

i. Types of Goods

The type of goods to be taken as a security should be considered because perishable goods are not usually recommended to be taken as a security whereas non perishable goods are highly recommended.

ii. Ready Market

[75] Black. J (2002). *Oxford Dictionary of Economics*. USA. Oxford University press. P.199
[76] English Sales of Good Act, 1893. Section 62(1)
[77] Adesanya, M. O and Ooyede, E.O (2004). *Business Law in Nigeria*. Ibadan. Evans Brothers Ltd. P.88-89

This factor is also considered key because the demand for such goods must be relatively stable as this will further makes realization in case of default simple.

iii. Price

it is very rare for one to detach price from goods. Accepting goods as a security the price of such goods should be relatively stable or increasing in nature as this will further add value to the security in future.

iv. Cost

Just as how price cannot be separated from goods so also cost. For every goods produced, cost is involved in all its production process. Thus, the cost of producing such goods should be considered in order to avoid been over inflated by the borrower.

v. Equity

This has to do with the customer stake/commitment in the transaction because in absence of it, the borrowers commitment will be very low and as a result most banks has set up a benchmark or standard of customers contribution ranging from 70:30 but which also depends on customers' ability as some might contribute 50:50 etc.

vi. Regulation or Policies

This factor is very important in accepting goods as a security for bank lending. Banks are to ensure that such goods are not listed in the contra-band goods, the exporter/importer is duly licensed by the appropriate authority as failure to observe such will make such security null and void.

vii. Title

Here, we are to take into consideration the interest on the goods. Banks are to ensure that the title to the goods is not ambiguous, not encumbered. They are also to ensure full payment of the goods to the seller so that they can have full title over it because partial payment does not give the buyer title to the goods, thus it cannot be pledged. Just as it is obtain in the Ramalpa Case. But such is mostly averted as banks used letter of Credit most especially the confirmed type.

viii. Insurance

This is very important as the banks are to ensure that such goods is fully insured by a reputable insurance company against unforeseen circumstances and also it is advisable that the bank interest is noted as a first loss payee.

ix. Warehouse

This has to do with where the goods will be kept pending full recovery. The goods should be warehoused in a government bonded warehouse pending the sale and which is to be in the banks name. Most a times the banks has accredited warehouse agent which is saddled with such responsibilities.

x. Performance History or Record

This has to do with the track performance of the borrower. His experience in the line of business, his market share could be summed up as an appraisal to be accepted because it is not always advisable to offer such to customers that are first timers in such line of business considering the risk surrounded with it.

However, under this form of security arrangement, there are certain security documents which are to be duly executed by the borrower. Amongst such are; Stock hypothecation and Trust Receipt.

i. Stock or Letter of Hypothecation

This is called letter of Lien, letter of pledge etc. it is means through which a lender (Bank) can be better secured in cases where the goods are to be left in the actual or constructive possession of the borrower[78]. In other words, it is document which gives the bank charge over the goods but the goods still remains in the position of the debtor. But this kind of security is not always advisable because the bank has no control over it and considering its mobility nature.

Under this arrangement, goods are released in piecemeal to the customer for sale while proceeds realized from such sale are credited into customer's account pending approval to further release goods. This process continues until full

[78] Igweike, K. I. Law of Banking and Negotiable Instruments. Africana First Press Limited.Lagos.2004.P.185

payment of the debt but upon default, the bank has the power of sale of such goods in order to offset the outstanding debt.

In addition, letter of hypothecation ranks the bank as a secured creditor in event of bankruptcy of the borrower. The case of Loyds bank Ltd vs. Bank of Amene National Trust and Savings association[79] can be used to buttress this fact.

4.6.1 Advantages of Letter of Hypothecation

i. In case of bankruptcy, the bank is ranked as a secured creditor.

ii. It gives the bank the right to sell upon default by the borrower.

iii. The formalities involved are very simple.

iv. It also gives the bank the right of lien over such goods.

v. Goods are been realized in piecemeal by the banks agent which gives the bank a safe haven to control and monitor, thus diversion in any form is minimized.

4.6.2 Disadvantages of Letter of Hypothecation

i. It involves huge cost to administer such as warehousing charges, agent fee, insurance charges etc.

ii. There exists the possibility of diversion of funds.

iii. The fact that the bank is not in physical control of all the goods, it is expose to tendency of customer reallocation overnight which may cause havoc to the facility.

iv. There exist a tendency of conspiracy between the warehouse agent and the borrower and bank officer.

ii. Trust Receipt

[79] Harbury India Rubber Comb. Co V Martin (1902) 1K.B 778; Davys Buswell (1914) 2K.B 47; Goulston Discount Co. Ltd v Clark (1967) 2 Q.B.493

Trust receipt refers to a written legal document binding a bank and a borrower whereby the latter promises to hold the financed item or goods for the benefit of the former pending the time the debt is paid off. Trust receipt is closely related to Import finance Facility where by the goods imported is the subject of security.[80]

Under this arrangement, the borrower undertakes to pay all the proceeds generated from sale of such goods and the borrower is considered as a trustee or agent for the bank. This form of security is not reliable as there exist the possibility of diversion of funds by the borrower as the goods is under his control. However, due to its flaws or loopholes it is recommended to customers with high integrity and good credit and track record.

Trust receipt has been in existence but is now fully incorporated into the government by Article 9 of the uniform Commercial Code, which has to do with secured transactions. This form of security is preferable for financing consumer durable such as automobile, Television etc.

Advantages of Trust Receipt

i. It provides greater security for the lender than floating lien.

ii. It does not involve cost of perfection.

iii. It gives the bank the power to repossess upon default.

iv. The formalities involve in trust receipt is very simple.

Disadvantages of Trust Receipt

i. There are possibilities of diversion of funds by the borrower.

ii. Since, the bank has no physical control over goods, it is expose to many risk such borrower may relocate overnight which might jeopardize the repayment

[80] Onyiriuba Leo . *Analysing and Managing Risk of Bank Lending*. NFS Data Bureau Ltd. Lagos Second Edition. 2008.P388-389

Having considered the security document involved in accepting goods as a security, it is also pertinent to dwell into the pros and cons in accepting goods as a security against bank lending.

4.6.4 Advantages of Goods as a Security

i. It is a security that can eat its cake and have it. Thus, it is a self liquidating security.

ii. The formalities involved in taking goods as a security is less cumbersome compared to landed properties.

iii. There exist a ready or organized market, hence makes realization simple.

iv. Cost of perfection of title or expense under this form of security arrangement is less expensive.

v. The existence of equity contribution by the borrower for the gods pledge will increase the sense of comfort on the part of the borrower, thus issue of default will be consider as remote.

4.6.5 Disadvantages of Goods as a Security

i. Market or price fluctuation may affect the value of such goods.

ii. It is only limited to certain types of goods mostly durable goods.

iii. It involves a lot of a expenses ranging from warehouse, agent fee and insurance fee etc.

iv. The fact that the bank is not in physical control of the goods, customer can outsmart the bank.

v. Apart from the price or demand other factors like evaporation, rotten may also affects the value of goods.

vi. Despite the fact that the goods are insured, payment of claim has been a major problem amongst insurance company.

4.7 Cash Deposit as a Security

Cash is considered as the safest security that can be pledge as against borrowing by banks. Cash in this case refers to credit balance in an account. It could be a savings, current or fixed deposit account. Cash when pledge as collateral, the borrower cannot have access to it until full payment of the debt. Thirty party customers can also pledge such security on behalf of the borrower.

Cash is the most liquid and releasable form of security but banks still has bench marks for accepting it. This further depends on the credit policy of such banks. Some banks might have set 120% as the margin which implies that the cash should be 120% of the facility amount so as to take care of the problem of unforeseen circumstances in the near future.

In order to fit in cash as collateral banks has succeeded in developing credit products like cash back facilities. Accepting foreign currency as a deposit to be pledge as collateral is not advisable due to risk of exchange rate fluctuations which may have effect on the value of the security.

4.7.1 Advantages of Cash as a Security

i. Realization is very simple as no cost is involved due to the fact that the borrower has executed the letter of lien and set off which empower the bank.

ii. The formalities involved in its process are not cumbersome as compared to landed properties.

iii. Valuation problem is considered remote as it is already in monetary units.

iv. The value of it is relatively stable no matter the phase of business cycle encountered.

v. The cost of investigation of title, legal search, registration or perfection etc is not incurred in accepting this form of security.

4.7.2 Documentary Requirements

i. Letter of instruction from the borrower to place lien on account.

ii. Duly executed letter of lien and set off

iii. Board resolution authorizing the placing of lien- if borrower is a company and the company's MERMART allows for such.

iv. Duly executed deed of assignment in favour of the borrower if it is a third party

4.7.3 Determination of Cash as a Security

Cash as a form of security can be determined if the following events occurs in order to avoid the operations of the Clayton case against the bank.

i. Breach of the terms and conditions of the facility agreement by the borrower.

ii. Bankruptcy of the borrower or third party.

iii. Death of a borrower or third party- in case of an individual

iv. Notice of determination by the third party.

v. Mental incapacity of the borrower or third party.

4.8 Domiciliation of Payment as a Security

In every credit granted by the bank, there is generally an assumption of possible diversion of funds by the borrower but in order to mitigate against such assumption domiciliation of is normally executed.

Domiciliation of payment refers to a tripartite arrangement (bank, Borrower, third party) whereby the third party (Employer) undertakes to pay the sum due to the borrower directly to the bank until the facility amount is fully redeemed.

This form of security is mostly used in terms of contract financing or loan applicable to salary earners and is applicable to other forms of credit. It is considered as a source of repayment and it is mostly recommended to be accompanied with other collateral.

Under this arrangement, there exist certain factors to be put under consideration before accepting such type of security.

i. **Integrity of the Third Party:** That is the reason banks normally accept such from blue chip companies or government organization with good track record in terms of credit history or payment. That why most banks have developed the idea of counter party arrangement.

ii. **The Financial Strength of the Third party:** This is also relevant as the financial capacity goes a long way to determine the whether or not the agreed date of payment will be achievable or not.

4.8.1 Advantages of Domiciliation of Payment

i. Once executed by the third party, he is under a legal obligation to pay directly to the bank.

ii. Cost of perfection or valuation is not involved.

iii. The formalities involved is very simple

iv. The bank can sue for the debt via court assistance.

4.8.2 Disadvantages of Domiciliation of Payment

i. This form of security is not attached to any specific asset of the third party.

ii. In bankruptcy, the bank can only be proved as an unsecured creditor.

iii. Such security will be null and void if the borrower has no insurable interest in the life of the third party.

4.9 Negative Pledge as a Security

Negative pledge is an undertaken by the borrower that the asset has not and will not be pledged as security for another person.[81] Consequently, it prohibits the borrower from creating any security interest over its assets without the consent of the lender.

This form of security is acceptable from borrowers with good credit history, payment history and exercise high level of integrity. It is mostly acceptable from blue chips companies. In a Negative pledge, negative covenants are

[81] John E. I . "Practice of Banking" CIBN *Exam Distance Learning Pack.* PE III.. Accountancy Training and Publication Ltd. Lagos 2011. Pp. 125-147

embedded in order to ensure that bank exposure is minimized. Amongst such negative covenants in a loan agreement are as follows;

i. No disposing of asset

ii. No Mortgage or lien to be incurred

iii. No changes in the scope of project (in case of project finance)

iv. No repayment of any recognized debt unless to the lender on a parri passu basis.

v. No decrease in Net worth below an agreed level.

4.9.1 Advantages of Negative Pledge

i. It can be easily taken

ii. It is not expensive to perfect

iii. The lender can sue for its debt in case of default.

4.9.2 Disadvantages of Negative Pledge

i. This form of security is not attached specifically to any asset.

ii. The bank exposure is high as during liquidation because the unattached asset could be seize and disposed off by the liquidator.

iii. Any legal charge on those assets takes priority over the negative pledge.

iv. In case of bankruptcy, the bank can only be proved as an unsecured creditor.

v. Realization is difficult as it requires court assistance.

4.10 Letter of Comfort or Awareness

Letter of comfort refers to a written formal letter written by a reputable company to a lending institution acknowledging support of its subsidiary borrowing from the bank[82]. This form of security only creates moral obligation on the part of the issuer rather than a legal obligation which implies that it does not serve as a guarantee to its subsidiary in case of default.

In the nut shell, the letter of comfort only gives some sort of assurance to the lending institution that the borrower will not default in its repayment. Most company do not like to issue such letter unless necessary because if it is not properly drafted it could incur some liability on them.

Letter of comfort is usually prepared on the issuer letter headed paper duly signed under sealed by two directors or a director and the company secretary.

4.10.1 Advantages of Letter of Comfort

i. It can be easily taken

ii. Costs of valuation, perfection, investigation of title are not involved in this form of security.

iii. It gives some sort of assurance to the bank that the borrower will not default.

iv. It add more credentials to the credit profile of the borrower.

4.10.2 Disadvantages of Letter of Comfort

i. The issuer does not incur any legal obligation in case of default by the borrower.

ii. If there exist loopholes in its wording, it could incur some liability to the issuer and if it is to exonerate itself, some expenses will be incurred as legal expenses.

iii. It is neither attached to the asset of the borrower nor the issuer.

Amongst some of the documents that a bank will demand to support such loan applications are

[82] Onyiriuba Leo . *Analysing and Managing Risk of Bank Lending*. NFS Data Bureau Ltd. Lagos Second Edition. 2008. P. 389

i. Last audited financial statement

ii. Cash flow projection for the years ahead

iii. Last management accounting report.

4.11 *Other Types of Securities (Collateral)*

4.11.1 Equipment Lease Agreement

Lease is a contractual arrangement calling for the lessee (user) to pay the lessor (owner) for the use of an asset.[83] This is usually over an agreed period of time and the amount payable by the lessee is called lease Rentals.

Lease can be finance, Sales and Lease back, Operating and Leverage lease. Lease been a loan product is special because based on its features; the equipment financed serves as the security to the facility.

Under this arrangement, there exist also an equity contribution from the borrower may be 20%, 30% or above depending on the credit policy of the bank whereas the bank finance the outstanding amount. Here, the title of equipment financed lies with the bank until full redemption but in order to properly bind the parties involved there exist an agreement which is normally drafted and duly signed under sealed and delivered by parties involved.

Thus, the Equipment lease agreement refers to a document stating the terms and conditions of the lease. It normally contains the Parties involved, amount, duration, mode of repayment, rights of both parties etc. The fact that there exist no other collateral apart from the equipment financed,s the equipment lease agreement serves as the collateral to support the borrowing.

4.11.2 Assignment of Book Debts

A debt refers to money owned by one person or firm to another[84]. This debt arises when goods are delivered according to the order request but payment for such goods is pending.

[83] https://en.m.wikipedia.org/lease. Retrieved on 18/03/2017. 3:20pm

Assignment of book debts as a form of security against lending though it is very rare amongst banks in Nigeria considering the technicalities but it is mostly used in advanced countries like USA. It is seen as a bank creating debt upon debt.

However, for a bank or financial institution to accept assignment of book debts as a form of security it is either in form of factoring or invoice discounting services.

4.11.3 Factoring

This refers to the buying of debt due from another business customers and collecting them[85]. It can also be seen as a mechanism for managing, financing and collecting of receivable. Under this arrangement, the value of the total book debt is been assigned to the bank for onward lending of certain amount out of the book debt to the customer/borrower.

Thus, the bank assumes the responsibility of receiving or collecting the book debt from the third party or borrower customers in order to offset the credit facility.

Factoring can be done on the following forms:

i. **Non-Recourse factoring:** it is an arrangement whereby the factor buys the book debt out rightly and therefore accepts the risk of bad debts.

ii. **Recourse factoring:** it also involves the provision of similar services but under this arrangement the client guarantees that the debt sold will be paid.

iii. **Maturity factoring:** under this arrangement the factors pays for the debt which he purchases on the maturity date or on collection.

However, factoring is **beneficial** in the following ways

i. Credits are better controlled.

[84] Hartzell, D. Dictionary of Management. Ogun. Melrose Books and Publishing, 2011. P.100

[85] Black . J (2002). *Oxford Dictionary of Economics*. USA. Oxford University press. P.169

ii. It improves the liquidity of the company via recovery of debts.

iii. In lieu of item 2, they have the ability to pay creditors as at when due.

Also, the **disadvantages** of such services are as follows:

i. Loss of goodwill

ii. Complains from customer due to the approach adopted by the factor in the recovering process.

4.11.4 Invoice Discounting

Under this arrangement, the borrower obtain credits funds by selling off its invoice books debts up to an agreed limit to the bank or a finance company at a discount for immediate payment.

4.11.1.1 Advantages of Assignment of Book Debts

i. The bank earns additional income from the security

ii. The fact that the banks buys the invoice debt on a discount, there exist a tendency of recovering more than the purchase price.

iii. Cost of perfection is not involved as compared to other forms of securities.

4.11.1.2 Disadvantages of Assignment of Book Debt

i. The cost of realization is sometimes expensive.

ii. There exist tendencies that some debts may not be recovered which will jeopardize the value of the security.

iii. Its process and formalities is sometimes time consuming.

iv. It could sometimes lead to bad publicity on the part of the bank in the process of recovery of such debt which on the whole will affect the corporate image of the bank

4.11.5 Bonds

Bond is a debt instrument in which an investors loans money to an entity (typically corporate or government) which borrows the funds for a definite period of time at a variable or fixed interest rate.[86]

Bonds are debt security in which the issuer owes the holder a debt and is oblige to pay them interest or to pay the principal at the maturity date. Under this arrangement, the holder of the bond is the creditor; the issuer of the bond is the borrower. Bond may be issued by firms, financial institution or government.

Bond has the following features:-

i. **Bonds covenants:** This involves the rules that specify the rights of the lender and the restriction of the borrower.

ii. **Option:** This permits both buyers and sellers to terminate the agreement.

iii. **Maturity:** this is the maximum length of time the borrower has to pay off the bond principal in full. In most cases, it is usually below 30years.

iv. **Price:** This is the amount at which a bond sell particular in relation to the principal.

v. **Face Value:** it is called Par Value. It is normally issued at N1000 and interest is paid on the face value.

A bond issued by government, the tendency of default is very minimal compared to bonds issued by private companies. Private companies bonds are called Debenture which has been earlier discussed. Under this arrangement, the bond holders can pledge their certificate as collateral for the loans or advances and upon default the lender can go ahead to sell it off on the floor of the market. Thus bond can be easy realizable considering it.

4.11.6 Money Market Instruments as a Security

Money market is a market where by short fund are raised. This market utilizes certain instrument in raising such funds which can also be used as securities for bank lending. We shall consider few of such instruments are:-

4.11.6.1 Treasury Bills

[86] www.investopedia.com/term/b/bond.asp. Retrieved on 18/03/2017. 4:50pm

They are promissory note issued by the apex bank on behalf of the federal Government with maturity period within 91day and its default free. In other words, there are mere IOU's governments used to borrow for short period pending the collections of its revenue[87]. Holders of this bills are issued certificate with describes details of their holdings. Such certificate can suffice as collateral for loans.

4.11.6.2 Treasury Certificate

They are similar to Treasury bills. Treasury Certificates are issued at par or face value. Fixed interest rates are paid to holders which are called coupon rate. They are considered as medium term government securities with maturity between 1-2years. Holders are issued certificate as evidence of their holdings which can also be used as securities for lending.

4.11.6.3 Commercial Paper

They are considered as short term promissory note issued by large corporations with maturity period ranging from 50 to 270days at various denominations. They are issued at a discount from face value and reflect prevailing market interest rates.

Commercial paper is considered as unsecured debt because it is not usually backed by any form of collateral[88] rather it is backed only by an issuing bank or company promise to pay the face amount on the maturity date specified on the note[89]. Buyers of Commercial paper are financial institutions, wealthy individuals, blue chips companies and money market funds etc

4.11.6.3 Certificate of Deposit

A certificate of deposit is a promissory note issued by a bank. They are considered savings certificate with maturity fixed date, specified fixed interest rate[90]. Certificate of deposit is a debt instruments that have a low risk. Holders of such deposit are issued a certificate which shows details of their holdings, thus such certificate can be pledge as securities against loan.

---

[87] Anyannwu, C (1993). *Monetary Economics. Theory, Policy and Institutions.* Onitsha. Hybrid Publishers Ltd. Pp.158-160
[88] www.investopedia.com/terms/c/commercialpaper.asp. Retrieved 21/03/2017. 08:56am
[89] https://en.wikipedia.org/wiki/Commercial_paper. Retrieved 21/03/20117. 09:05am
[90] www.investopedia.com/terms/c/certificateofdeposit.asp. Retrieved 21/03/2017. 09:30am

Chapter Five: Overview of Islamic Banking

5.0 Introduction

Islamic banking as the name implies got its pedigree from Islam and in lieu of that, it can be refer to as a financial institution whose statutes, rules and procedures expressly state its commitment to the principles of Islamic shariah (jurisprudence) and forbids of the receipt and paying interest on any transaction. This definition is well accepted by the General Secretariat of the Organization of Islamic Conference and the Islamic Development bank[91]. It can also be defined as a model of non-interest banking that is consistent with the principles of Islamic Shariah which is also known as *Fiqh Al-Mu'amalat* (Jurisprudence of Commercial transaction).

The rules and practices of *Fiqh Al-Mu'amalat* emanated from the Quran and the Sunnah, and other secondary sources of Islamic law such as opinions collectively agreed among Shariah scholars (*ijma*), analogy (*qiyas*) and personal reasoning (*ijtihad*). However, from the definition above we can deduced that amongst the major contending issue surrounding Islamic banking is that the Shariah law prohibits the receipt and payment of interest on money lent which is often referred to as *Riba* or *Usury*.

Riba literally means "Increase in" or "addition to" anything[92]. As a result, it can be seen as an excess over the capital lent or a fixed return for the use of money. The argument against *Riba* or Usury is that money is not used as a commodity with which to make profit but that it should be earned on goods and services only, not on control of money itself. In essence, money has no intrinsic utility.[93] it is only a medium of exchange.

However, *Riba* exists in a loan contract where the lender charges an additional amount on the principal and also in an exchange contract where commodities are exchanged at counter values. *Riba* may arise in different forms. According to a hadith of the Prophet (pbuh) there are seventy-three types of *Riba*. [94]Due to lack of a better word, some tend to translate *Riba* as usury.

---

[91] Tajur Islam, "Mechanics of Islamic Banking", In *Islamic Banking; How far Have we Gone*. Edited by Pramanik H A, IIUM Press, Malaysia. 2009: p. 126

[92] Muhammad Musleh, "Meaning of *Riba*", In *Islamic Banking; How far Have we Gone*. Edited by Pramanik H A, IIUM Press, Malaysia. 2009: p. 28

[93] Usmani T. M (2010). *An Introduction to Islamic Finance*. New Delhi. India Adam Publisher and Distributors. P.19

[94] Ibn Majah, v.2, p.764:2274

Usury generally, however, implies only the excessive form of increase, whereas *Riba* implies all forms of increase in a loan contract. Similarly, translating *Riba* as interest does not provide a comprehensive meaning of *Riba* as the word interest captures only a type of *Riba*, not all forms of it[95]. Traditionally, interest only refers to the *Riba* in a loan contract and this form of *Riba* is more relevant to the present day banking system.

The origin of Islamic banking can be traced to Egypt when in 1963 the Mit Ghamr Saving bank in the Northern Delta region of the Nile which was established by a renowned Economist Ahmad El-Naggar. Islamic banking is now considered as a well known term and has emerged as one of the most important and fast growing industry worldwide with over 500 Islamic institutions in more than 75 countries[96].

However, this form of banking is branded for its interest free concept and operates in many countries including Bahrain, Pakistan, Jordan, Iran, Sudan, United Kingdom, Singapore, Malaysia, Bangladesh and Saudi Arabia etc. The Islamic banking sector has been in an upward trajectory, evidenced by its asset double digit Compound Annual Growth Rate (CAGR) of 17% between 2009 and 2013.[97]

The Islamic banking sector is estimated to be worth USD1.496 trillion as at first half of 2015 having grown from USD1.476 trillion as at first half in 2014[98] with about 38Million customers globally[99]. Despite, this enormous growth in asset, it still represent 1% [100]of the total world asset of about USD256 trillion[101].

In addition, the industry asset is heavily concentrated in the Middle East and Asia countries[102]. The Gulf Corporation Countries (GCC) region accounts for about 40% of the total global Islamic banking asset, the Middle East and North Africa (Excluding GCC's) region accounts for about 41%. This milestone was achieved largely due to Iran's fully

---

[95] Engku Ali, E.R.A and P. Odiermo, H. S, 2008. Essential Guide to Takaful (Islamic Insurance). Malaysia: CERT; In https://islamicaccountingandfinance.wordpress.com/2015/07/29/*Riba*-bank-interest-and-islamic-banking-a-summarised-response-to-fundamental-questions/. Retrieved 02/01/2016,3:38pm

[96] Ernest and Young Report (2013) "Young World Islamic Banking CompetitiveReport, 2013-14": 12-13.

[97] Islamic Finance Service Board (2015): *Islamic Financial Services Industry Stability Report*:7-76

[98] Islamic Finance Service Board (2016): Islamic Financial Services Industry Stability Report:7-22

[99] Ernest and Young Report (2013) "Young World Islamic Banking Competitive Report, 2013-14": 12-13.

[100] Economist (2014)" Islamic Finance; Big Interest no Interest" The Economist Newspaper Limited. Sept 13, 2014.

[101] Credit Suisse (2016)" Global Wealth Report" Switzerland. Research Institute. Thought leadership from Credit Suisse Research and the world's foremost expert. P.3

[102] Kammer, A, Norat M, Pinon M, Prasad A, Towe C, Zeidaine, Z and IMF Staff Team (2015). Islamic Finance: opportunities, Challenges and policy Options. IMF Staff Discussion Note :8-11and 26

Shariah compliant banking sector. Asia rank third representing 14% share in the global total Islamic banking asset. The contribution from other region, like Europe and Sub-Saharan Africa remain very low[103].

This form of banking system gives emphasis to mutual assistance through trading with its clients or to engaging in trading directly. But in doing so, it operates according to certain principles.

5.1 Principles of Islamic Banking

5.1.1 Prohibition of Interest:

This is considered as one of the core principle of Islamic banking. This entails that any predetermined return over and above the actual amount of the principal loaned is prohibited. But, Islam allows only one kind of loan which is called *Qard-el-hassan* (Good loan). It is seen as a type of loan whereby the lender does not charge any interest or additional amount over the money lent. The prohibition of interest derives its source from both the Holy Quran and the Sunnah of the prophet. The Holy Quran states that;

"*Those who eat Riba (Usury) will not stand (on the day of resurrection) except like the standing of a person beaten by shaitan (Satan) leading him to insanity. That is because they said; Trading is only like Riba'' whereas Allah has permitted trading and forbidden Riba; so who so ever recieves admonition from his lord and stops eating Riba (usury) shall not be punished for the past, his case is for Allah (to Judge) but who ever returns to Riba, such are the dwellers of the fire- they will abide therein.''* ***(Q 2:275).***

Likewise, in the bible same prohibition is also made in the following verses Luke 6:34-35, Psalm 15:5, Deut 23:19 etc.

5.1.2 Profit and Loss Sharing:

Islamic banking is based on the principle of profit and loss sharing which depicts a divergence from the conventional system of banking. This means that lender and the user of the funds must share in the profit or loss from the investment/venture for which the money was lent according to the agreed ratio or capital contribution if

[103] Islamic Finance Service Board (2016): Islamic Financial Services Industry Stability Report:7-22

funds are invested under the *Shirkah* agreement. This principle discourages one to be a creditor. The central juristic principle in the Shariah that informs our concept of risk-sharing states: "*al ghunm bil ghurm,*" meaning "there is no return without risk." (Ethica Institute of Islamic Finance, 2013)

5.1.3 Gambling, Uncertainty and Speculation (*Maysir*) are Prohibited

Islamic Banking has prohibits transaction involving gambling. As it is clearly spelt out in the glorious Quran, in Suratul Maidah which states that:-

O you who believe! Intoxicants (All kinds of alcoholic drinks) and gambling and Al-ansab and Al-Azlam (arrow for seeking luck of decision) are abomination of shaitan (Satan) handiwork. So avoid (strictly all) that abomination in order that you may be successful. ***(Q5:90).***

Also in **Q2:219** which states are follows:-

They ask you (O Muhammad) concerning alcoholic drink and Gambling, say: "*In them is a great sin and (some) benefits for men, but the sin of them is greater than their benefit." And they ask you what they ought to spend. Say" that which is (spare) beyond your needs". Thus Allah makes clear to you his laws in order that you may give you thought.*

In fact, Gambling is seen as Gharar in a worst case scenario because it is seen as a game of chance. In addition, the principle also demands that any transaction entered into should be freed from uncertainty risk and speculation. That is, parties involved should have an in-depth knowledge of the transaction dynamics. For example, investment in futures and options are prohibited Islamically.

5.1.4 Unethical Businesses is Prohibited

Islamic banking is based on the principle which prohibits investments in unethical businesses or prohibited commodities. That is it only supports practices or products that are in line with the sharia law. For example trading in alcohol, pork is prohibited as stated in Suratul Maidah

"Forbidden to you (for food) are; Al-maitah (the dead animals-cattle- beast not slaughtered), blood, the flesh of swine, and that which Allah's name has not been mentioned while slaughtering (that which has been slaughtered as

a sacrifice for others than Allah, or has been slaughtered for idols) and that which has been killed by strangling, or by a violent blow, or by a headlong fall or by goring of horns- and that which has been partly eaten by wild animal- unless you are able to slaughter it (before its death)- and that which is sacrificed (slaughtered on an- nusub (Stone altars). Forbidden also is to use arrow seeking luck or decision; (all) that is fisqun (disobedience of Allah and sin). This day, those who disbelieved have given up all hope for your religion; so fear them not, but fear me. This day I have perfected your religion for you, completed my favour upon you and have choosen for you islam as your religion. But as for him who is forced by severe hunger, with no inclination to sin (such can eat these above mentioned meats), then surely, Allah is oft-forgiving, Most merciful". **(Q5:3).**

Also, in **Q5:90**, the same prohibition has also been pronounced. Likewise in the Bible similar prohibition has been made in the following verses; Isaiah 5:22, Habakkuk 2:15, Proverbs 20:1, Deuteronomy 21:18-21, Luke 12:45-47, Leviticus 11:7, Isaiah 65:3-4,66:17 and Deuteronomy 14:8. As a result of this, Islamic banking investment portfolios in those areas have been prohibited out rightly no matter how profitable it is.

Chapter Six: Sources of Funds for Islamic Banking

6.1 Introduction

Islamic bank needs funds to operate its activities just like the conventional banks because without funds, such organization will not be in existence, so therefore funds are considered as the blood of every organization. Thus, we shall trace the source of funds available for Islamic banks. The available sources of funds as internal and external sources; capital, Retained earnings Reserves, Deposits collected from customers, Deposit from other Islamic banks, Islamic Investment funds, Placement from Bank treasury etc[104].

6.2 Internal Sources

i. Capital

Capital for the Islamic financial institutions and especially banks is the insurance (safety value) that absorbs the expected loses which may occur in the future. In addition, capital is the basic source of the funds to start the activity. Also, capital is the safety and protection and the source of trust for the depositors[105].

ii. Reserves

They are the funds that are set aside from the benefits of the bank in a form of legal or special reserve in order to support the financial position of the bank. The basic laws of the banks include the bases of the legal reserve formation. Their formation often stops when they reach a specific ratio of the capital of the bank. Islamic banks forms different reserves categories required to support their financial positions keep the safety of their capitals and maintain the stability of the values of their deposits and the balance of their earnings.[106]

iii. Retained Earnings

They refer to the portion of the net income which is retained by the corporation to reinvest them afterwards to support the financial position of the bank. This does not include the profits that are decided to be distributed and

[104] Abdulkarim, A.S (2011)." Sources and Application of Funds in Non Interest Banks Regime. *Central Bank of Nigeria Bullion*. 35(3): 3-5 ; El-Seoudi. M, Mohd, N. M, Amir, H.M, Zaini, N, Shofian Ahmad, M, N, and Ahmad Dahlan, S (2012). "Sources of funds and invested in Malaysian Islamic Banks" Advances in Natural and Applied Sciences, 6(7): 1130-1135

[105] Al-'Awadi, R. S, (2009). *Encyclopedia of Islamic Economy* , 1st edition, Cairo: House of As-Salaam.

[106] Shihaatah, S (1977). *Islamic banks* , Jeddah: House of Ash-Shurooq

were not asked by some shareholders yet[107]. When the Islamic bank retains some profits, this does not conflict with the rulings of the Islamic Shariah because it (i.e. the bank) acts as a *Mudaarib* (speculator) with the money of the depositors. Therefore, the Islamic bank can withhold a specific part of the profits to face what it may experience of unusual conditions.

6.3 External Sources

i. Deposits Collected from Customers

Deposits collected from customers are also as one of the sources of funds available to Islamic banks and at the same time it can be referred to as the types of accounts been operated by Islamic banks. Deposit in Islamic law means that a person entrust his resources to someone whom he trusted will take care of it under the condition that what is to be kept can be possessed and looked after.

Money meant as deposit cannot be used under Islamic law, but if it will be used and be refunded in the same amount it is known as loan in Islamic law and not a deposit. Since a deposit is a trust, the person entrusted will not be asked to repay (in case of any calamity that befall the wealth), unless it is due to his negligence or he uses it; In Islamic banking each customer is a partner with the Islamic banks. This relationship is classified as the *Musharakah* partnership.

Profits resulting from the accounts are divided between parties. An Islamic banks receives a certain percentage of the net profits, as a return for the amounts deposited in different investment accounts as its share, being a *Musharakah,* as agreed between the customers, who is the investment account holder.

[107] Abdel Haady, Ahmad, Nabeel, 1985. *Methodological and scientific aspects in administering funds of the commercial banks* , Cairo: House of As-Salaam.

6.3.1 Types of Accounts

6.3.1.1 Current Account

Current accounts are interest- free accounts which are opened by companies, firms and individuals. Under this form of account, the bank guarantee the return of principal deposits and it is based on the principle of *Al-wadiah* or Guarantee Trust.

Under this arrangement, Islamic bank has the right to invest the funds it is holding in current account without the customer bearing any loss. For this reason, the customer does not get any profit on this type of account, but he also does not bear any loss.

6.3.1.1 Saving Account

These types of account are opened by individuals only as companies and firms are not entitled to open such account. This form of accounts allows the account holder to place funds in a safe environment till such time when they wish to withdraw them. Profits and losses under such accounts accrue on the minimum monthly balance.

Profits are paid according to the percentage from the net profit of the bank as agreed, or losses are deducted, after expiry of the financial year. Savings deposits are collected under various principles; firstly, *Al-wadiah*- This form of account has similar features to a current account but it does not have any cheque. Under strict principle of *al-wadiah* the bank is not supposed to give any return, but if the bank decides, such return is given as *hibah* or a gift.

Secondly, *Al-wadiah* and *Mudharabah*- It is seen as an alternative to *al-wadiah* savings where returns are not given. A hybrid of *al-wadiah* and *mudharabah* (loss or loss sharing principle) deposit product was introduced. Under this principle, certain portion of profits derived from the *mudharabah* investment is shared with the depositors. Lastly, *Mudharabah*- Under this principle, depositors (Investors) will be entitle for some profits based on an agreed profit sharing ratio.

6.3.1.2 General Investment Account

These types of account are also called deposit with authorization. This is an investment account with a pre-determined profit sharing ratio and maturity period. General Investment depositors are contracted under the *mudharabah* idea, where depositors and the banks agree at the time of placement, the profit sharing ratio and the placement period. Depositors who place their funds under longer period will be paid higher profits than depositors who place their fund on a shorter period.

6.3.1.3 Specific Investment Account

It is sometimes refers to as deposits without authorization. This is a unique investment accounts where depositors will be advised on where their funds will be invested, the minimum amount that they can be invest, the returns on the investment and as well as the risk associated with such investment. Returns on this form of account are very high so therefore most depositors are keen to place their funds under such account.

Under this type of account, any loss from the investment/project will be borne entirely by the depositor. Funds under this account are use majorly on real estate related investment and depositors that operate this type of account are by invitations only.

ii. Islamic Investment funds:

Islamic Investment Funds is seen as a joint pool where in investors contributes their surplus money for the purpose of its investment to earn *halal* profits in strictly conformity with the precepts of Islamic shariah[108].

Under this arrangement a certificate (document) is normally issued as evidence of ownership which depicts the investors amount of subscription whereas profit are distributed on pro-rata basis which is to be agreed upon at the point the contract is made, in this case the profit and loss sharing principle is adopted.

iii. Placement from Bank Treasury

This is also considered as a source of fund available to Islamic banks which are supported by the money market. The money market is used by the Islamic banks as a means for borrowing and lending at a short term from several days to a year.

[108] Usmani, T. M (2010). *An Introduction to Islamic Finance*. New Delhi. India Adam Publisher and Distributors:27-198

This could involve the use of *Al-mudaraba* Interbank Investment, Government Investment Certificate, Islamic Accepted bills, Bankers acceptances, Repurchase agreement and Islamic Negotiable Instruments etc.

iv. Deposit from other Banks

It is also considered as a source of funds available to Islamic banks because it has been a practice amongst banks be it conventional or Islamic banks to place funds amongst themselves for investable or lending purposes.

Chapter Seven: Financing Modes in Islamic Banking

7.0 Introduction

Remember Allah says in the Glorious Quran;

"O *ye who believe! squander not your wealth among yourselves in vanity, except it be a trade by mutual consent"*. ***(Q4:29).***

It be deduced from the above verse that Allah has encouraged we mankind to invest our wealth but such investment should not be contrary to the shariah. Hence, for Islamic bank to survive as an entity and perform its role properly as financial intermediaries, it has to engage into various form of investments or business which are shariah compliance either directly or indirectly such as engaging into partnership business, setting up business ventures, purchasing of shares in companies etc so as to generate income. Thus, to facilitate the realization of these objectives necessitate the need for the development for various credit products that could the need of customers.

7.1 Lending Modes in Islamic Banking

However, there are different ways by which Islamic bank engages into the business of lending. Amongst which are:

i. Murabahah – Sales Contract

ii. *Mudarabah*- Part financing

iii. *Musharakah*- Partnership

iv. *Ijarah* – Rent or Lease

v. *Tawarruq*-Overdraft facilities

vi. Istisna'a

vii. Bai Salam

viii. *Bai' al' inah* – Sales and Buy-back agreement)

ix. *Bai'bithaman* (Deferred payment Sale)

x. *Bai' Mujjal* (Credit Sale)

7.1.1 Murabahah

The Concept emanates from the Arabic word ''*rabh*'' which means profit. It is defined as the sale of goods at a price, which includes a profit margin agreed by both parties. Under this arrangement, the purchase and selling price, other costs and the profit margin must be clearly stated at the time of the sales agreement.

Murabahah can simply be referred to as sale but the distinguishing feature of it from other kinds of sale is that it informs the buyer of the cost and how much profit to charge in addition to the cost and if otherwise then it should be on *MUSAWAMMAH* basis.

Murabahah sales are guided by the same conditions applied to general sales in shariah. Amongst the conditions are:-

i. The item must be in existence at the time of the transactions.

ii. The seller must be in ownership or have title to the item to be sold.

iii. The sale must be instant and absolute

iv. The item must have value

v. The item should not be amongst the prohibited commodities.

vi. The buyer should be able to identify the item to be purchase.

vii. The price and delivery of the item should be certain.

viii. The sale must be unconditional.

The basic **features** of *Murabahah* financing are as thus[109]

i. It is not a loan given on interest. It is the sale of a commodity for a deferred price which includes an agreed profit added to the cost.

[109] Usmani T. M (2010). *An Introduction to Islamic Finance*. New Delhi. India Adam Publisher and Distributors. Pp.95-103

ii. Being a sale and not a loan it should confirm with all the conditions necessary for a valid sale as stated above.

iii. *Murabahah* cannot be used as a mode of financing except where the client needs to actually purchase some commodities. It require real sales of some commodities and not merely advancing loans.

iv. The financier must have owned the commodity before he sells it to its clients.

v. The commodity must come into possession of the financier whether physical or constructive in the sense that the commodity must be in his high risk, though for a short period.

vi. The financier himself purchases the commodity and keeps it in his own possession or purchase the commodity though a third person appointed by him as a agent before he sell it to a customer.

vii. The sale cannot take place unless the commodities come into the possession of the seller but the seller can promise to sell even when the commodity is not in his possession.

viii. The institution may ask the client to furnish a security to its satisfaction for the prompt payment of the deferred price such as signing a promissory note or a bill of exchange, execution of hypothecation, lien or pledging of mortgage etc.

ix. In case of default by the buyer in the payment of the price at the due date, the price cannot be increased as any increment from the agreed price is not permitted but to ensure smooth recovery in case of default, the buyer may be asked to promise that he will donate some specified amount for charitable purpose in such a case, the seller receive such amount which shall not form part of his income but to utilize it for charitable purpose.

7.1.2 *Musharakah*

Musharakah literally means Sharing. This refers to a relationship between two parties or more whom pool their resources together to a business based on an agreed profit or Loss ratio. This is often used in investment projects, letters of credit, and the purchase or real estate or property. In the case of real estate or property, the banks assess an imputed rent and will share it as agreed in advance.

All providers of capital are entitled to participate in management, but not necessarily required to do so. *Musharakah* is synonyms to *shirkah* in Islamic *fiqh* and more precisely *Shirkat- ul- Amwal. Shirkah* is basically divided into two (2)[110]:-

a. ***Shirkat- ul-Milk*:-** it refers to a joint ownership of two or more persons in a particular property/asset.

b. ***Shirkat- ul-aqd:-*** it is seen as a partnership created by mutual contract. Shirkat ul-aqd is further divided into three(3) namely:-

i. ***Shirkat- ul- amwal:-*** This is where all the partners invest some capital into a commercial venture/enterprise

ii. ***Shirkat- ul-A'mal*:-** it is seen as where all partners jointly undertake to render some services for their customers and the fee charge is distributed according to an agreed ratio.

iii. ***Shirkat- ul-Wujooh*:-** In this case the partners has no investment. They only purchase the goods on a deferred price and sell them on the spot.

However, for *Musharakah* to be valid certain conditions need to be followed which are:-

i. The relationship established by both parties should be by mutual consent.

ii. The proportion of profit should be agreed at the time of effecting the contract

iii. The ratio of profit for each partners must be determined on the proportion to the actual profit accrued to the business and not in the proportion of capital contributed.

iv. The ratio of losses should be in proportion of their capital employed.

In addition, *Musharakah* can also be securitized in case of elephant projects where huge amount is required which a limited number of persons undertake. In this case each subscriber is issued a *Musharakah* certificate according to his investment whereby in the long run when the project has started acquiring non-liquid asset, these certificate can serve or treated as a negotiable instruments and can be traded in the secondary market but it cannot be traded in the market if all the asset of the *Musharakah* are still in liquid form.

[110] Usmani T. M (2010). *An Introduction to Islamic Finance*. New Delhi. India Adam Publisher and Distributors. P.31-45

In order to meet up changes in the financial world, a new concept of *Musharakah* was developed which is called the Diminishing *Musharakah.* It is mostly used in asset financing especially house financing. It is a system whereby the financier and his client participate either in joint ownership of the property or venture. In this case, the share of the financier will further be splitted and the client will purchase it one after the other until the financier is left with zero units which then make the client the sole owner.

In conclusion, *Musharakah* can be terminated based on the following grounds; every partner has the right to terminate the *Musharakah* upon notice, Death of partners and if one partner become insane or incapable of effecting financial transaction.

7.1.3 *Mudarabah*

"*Mudarabah*" is a special kind of partnership business. This is a contract between persons in which one person gives the other a sum of money with the aim investing it in a commercial venture/enterprise based on an agreed in profit ratio. Under this arrangement the capital owner is refer to as *"rabb-ul-mal",* while the management and work is left to the other person who is called *"Musharakah".* In the nutshell, it is seen as partnerships where the bank contributes 100% of the capital and the customer contributes its expertise.

Mudarabah can be restricted or unrestricted. In a case of a restricted *mudarabah* which is also called *al- mudarabah al- muqayyadah*, the *rabb-ul-mal* may specify a particular business for the *Musharakah* where as in the case of unrestricted *mudarabah*, the *Musharakah* is at liberty to invest the funds in whatever business he wishes but it should be in compliance with the shariah[111]. This is also refer to as al- *mudaraba al- mutlaqh. Mudaraba* can be used in Short/medium/long term financing, Project financing, SME set up, Import financing. LC's, Export (Pre-shipment Financing, Working Capital Financing.

However for a *mudarabah* to be valid certain conditions needs to be followed. Amongst which are :-

i. The capital should be in cash and not debt

[111] Usmani T. M (2010). *An Introduction to Islamic Finance*. New Delhi. India Adam Publisher and Distributors. Pp.47-92

ii. The capital should be known

iii. The capital should be given to the *Musharakah* in person

iv. There must be an agreed profit sharing ratio

v. The Loss of the business shall be borne by the *rabb-ul-mal* alone

vi. The capital should consist of paper money (Dirhams, Dinars etc) as *mudarabah* with goods is not permitted because it value fluctuates.

In order to mitigate against losses, the bank is entitle to request for a guarantor to guarantee its capital against loss due to shortcomings or violations as it's the basic rules guiding the trustworthy because *mudarabah* capital is held on the basis of trust. *Mudarabah* can be terminated either by the two parties but prior notice should be served to the other party before termination.

In conclusion, it is pertinent to highlight the **differences between *Musharakah* and *Mudarabah* mode of investments**

i. Investment in *Musharakah* comes from all partners while in the case of *Mudarabah* investment is the sole responsibility of rabb-ul-mal.

ii. All partners in the case of *Musharakah* can participate in the management of the business and can work for it whereas in the case of *mudarabah*, the rabb-ul-mal has no right to participate in the management.

iii. All partners share the losses to the extent of their investment but in the case of the *mudarabah*, the *Musharakah* losses is shared by the *rabb-ul-mal* alone

iv. The Liability of all partners is unlimited in *Musharakah* but in *Mudarabah* it is limited to his investment unless he has permitted the *Musharakah* to incur debt on his behalf.

v. In *Musharakah*, as soon as the partners mix up their capital all asset become jointly owned by all of them irrespective of their investment whereas in the case of *mudarabah* is different because all the goods purchase by the *Musharakah* are solely owned by the *rabb-ul-mal* and the *Musharakah* earn his share in the profit only when he sell the goods (Usmani,2010)

7.1.4 *Ijarah*

Ijarah as a concept refers to "rent out something". This means selling the benefit of use or service for a fixed price or wage. *Ijarah* can be can be defined as a contract granting use or occupation of an item of property during a specified period in the exchange for a specified rent.[112].

Ijarah is applicable to two scenerios[113]; employment of services and the use of asset or properties. *Ijarah* as applicable to services is seen as the employment of services of a person for a return (wages/salaries). Here, the employer of such services is called *Musta jir* while the employee is called *Ajir*. Whereas in the case of asset/properties it is refers to as Leasing; the usage of an asset/property for a time period in return for rent. Here the Lessor is called *Mujir* while the Lessee is called *Musta' ajir* and the rent payable is refer to as *Ujrah*.

Under this arrangement, the Bank makes available to the customer the use of service of assets / equipments such as plant, office automation, motor vehicle for a fixed period and price. There is Joint ownership between the bank and the client. The client rents it from the bank. Client enters into an agreement to buy the shares from the bank over an agreed timeframe.

Ijarah as to leasing has some guiding rules according to the Islamic Shariah (Usmani,2010),amongst which are:-

i. It is a contract that involves the transfer of an asset/property to another person for an agreed duration at an agreed return.

ii. The subject must have a valuable use.

iii. The subject must be consumable; the leasing of money, eatables, fuel etc is not allowed because one cannot utilize them unless it is consumed.

iv. The ownership of the property or asset remains with the lessor.

v. All liabilities attributable to the use of the property lies with the lessee while all liabilities referable to the property lies with the lessor.

---

[112] Abdul-Fattah, M and Shakier, R.Y (2006). *500 Questions and Answers on Islamic Jurisprudence.* Egypt. Dar Al-Manarah Publishers:351

[113] Usmani T. M (2010). *An Introduction to Islamic Finance*. New Delhi. India Adam Publisher and Distributors. Pp.157-181

vi. The lessee cannot use the property for any other purpose outside the specified one as agreed in the lease agreement.

vii. The lessee will be liable to the lessor resulting from the misuse or negligence on his part on the leased asset.

viii. The lessor bears the risk throughout the leased period apart from factor beyond the lessee control.

ix. A property jointly owned by more than one person can be leased out and the rental shall be distributed between them in accordance with the proportion of their shares in the property.

x. The leased asset must be fully identifiable by the parties.

xi. The lessor cannot independently increase the rent.

xii. It is permissible to pay the rental in advance.

xiii. The commencement period begins when the asset is delivered to the lessee.

xiv. The exist no charge for default but to avoid abuse, the lessee will be made to contribute certain percentage to the charity fund maintained by the lessor.

xv. If the lessee goes contrary to the lease agreement, the lessor has the right to terminate the lease contract if otherwise then mutual consent is required.

xvi. The lease property must be insured under the Islamic mode of takaful and the expense should be incurred by the lessor.

xvii. The lessee is not allowed to sublease the leased asset without the permission of the lessor.

xviii. The lessor has the right to sell the leased property to a third party whereby the relation between the lessor and lessee is done between the new owner.

xix. Assigning the lease without ownership on the leased asset for monetary consideration is not allowed.

Ijarah can be classified as follows; *Ijarah thumma al bai* (Hire purchase) and *ijarah –wal-iqtina.*

a. *Ijarah* Thumma Al Bai (Hire Purchase)

This is a form of complete lease and buyback transaction. Under this arrangement, the first phase of the contract is called an *Ijarah* which that outlines the terms for leasing or renting over a fixed period, and the second phase of the contract is a *Bai* that triggers a sale or purchase once the term of the *Ijarah* is complete.

For example, in a car financing facility, a customer enters into the first contract and leases the car from the owner (bank) at an agreed amount over a specific period. When the lease period expires, the second contract comes into effect, which enables the customer to purchase the car at an agreed to price. The bank generates a profit by determining in advance the cost of the item, its residual value at the end of the term and the time value or profit margin for the money being invested in purchasing the product to be leased for the intended term. The combining of these three figures becomes the basis for the contract between the Bank and the client for the initial lease contract.

b. *Ijarah*-Wal-Iqtina

Under this arrangement, the bank unilaterally undertakes that by the end of the lease period, the ownership in the asset would be transferred to the lessee. The undertaking or the promise does not become an integral part of the lease contract to make it conditional. The rentals as well as the purchase price are fixed in such manner that the bank gets back its principal sum along with profit over the period of lease. There exist two conditions guiding this form of *ijarah*

i. The promise should be unilateral and binding on the promissor only.

ii. The agreement of the *ijarah* (first phase) should not be subjected to the signing of the promise of sale or gift recorded in a separate document.

7.1.5 Tawarruq

Tawarruq means " to buy on credit and sell at spot value" [114]it is seen as a reverse murabaha for the purpose of acquiring cash through trade activities[115]. Thus, tawarruq is a financial instrument in which a buyer purchases a commodity from a seller on a deferred payment basis, and the buyer sells the same commodity to a third part on a spot payment basis.[116] This method is permissible according to the majority of the scholars, but they differed somehow as regards its name. For this sale to be acceptable, the buyer should fully possess the goods before selling them for the second time, and the second sale should be separate from the first sale.

[114] https:www.islamicbanker.com/education/tawarruq. Retrieved on 30/03/2017. 6:02am
[115] http://www.islamic-banking.com/glossory_t.aspx. Retrieved on 30/03/2017. 6:15am
[116] Feleel, J (2012). Islamic Finance for Dummies.Available at www.dummies.com/personal- finance/islamic-finance/reverse-murabaha-tawarruq-in-islamic-finance/ Retrieved on 30/03/2017. 6:30am

Furthermore, one should not sell the goods to the person from whom one bought them in principle if the cost of the goods is lesser than the price he bought them from him. These conditions are based on evidence." *Abdullah ibn Umar, may Allah be pleased with him, narrated that the prophet (SAW), prohibited selling the goods unless one has fully taken possession of it before hand.*'' **(Abu Daawood)**

7.1.6 Istisna'a

This is a form of sales transaction with immunity; that is it does not comply with the rules guiding sales. *Istisna'a* is a sales transaction where a commodity is sold before it comes into existence.[117]It can also be defined as a contract for the acquisition of manufactured goods, by specification or order, where the price is paid gradually in accordance with the progress of the job. The payment of an *Istisna'a* may be made in advance or instalments or in a lump sum at the end of the period.

Istisna'a can be used for financing certain transaction especially in the house finance sector, project financing such as building a bridge or a highway. The modern BOT (Buy Operate and Transfer) agreement may also be formalized on the basis of istina'a.

Under this arrangement, it is paramount that the price is fixed with the consent of the parties and that necessary specification of the commodity (intended to be manufactured) is fully settled between them before the manufacturing commences. Also, any party to the contract has the right to terminate the contact after giving notice but if he commences the work the contract cannot be cancelled unilaterally.

7.1.7 Bai Salam

Bai salam means a contract in which advance payment is made for goods to be delivered later on. It can also be refer to a as sale whereby the seller undertakes to supply some specified goods to the buyer at a future date in exchange of an advance price fully paid at spot.[118] This form of transaction also breaches the rules guiding sales. Here, the price is cash but the supply of the purchased goods is deferred. The buyer is called *Rabb-us-salam*, the seller is *muslam*

[117] Usmani T. M (2010). *An Introduction to Islamic Finance*. New Delhi. India Adam Publisher and Distributors. Pp.195

[118] Usmani T. M (2010). *An Introduction to Islamic Finance*. New Delhi. India Adam Publisher and Distributors. Pp.157-181

ilaih, the cash price is called *ra'sul mal* and the purchased commodity is term *muslam fih*. For *Bai Salam* to be valid, it has some principle guiding its operations (Usmani,2010):

i. The buyer must pay the price in full to the seller at the time of effecting the contract.

ii. This form of transaction is only effected on those commodity that the quality and quantity can be specified exactly. The objects of this sale are goods and cannot be gold, silver, or currencies based on these metals.

iii. The quality and quantity of the commodity must be clearly specified to avoid dispute.

iv. Salam cannot be effected on a particular commodity or product of a particular field or farms.

v. The exact date and place of delivery must be specified in the contract.

vi. Salam cannot be effected on commodities which can be delivered on spot.

vii. The commodity must be existing.

viii. The seller should have acquire the ownership of that commodity.

ix. Mere ownership is not enough, it should have come into possession of the seller physically or constructively.

Bai salam is beneficial because the bank may sell it through a parallel contract of salam for the same date of delivery. The differences in the prices serve as a profit. The shorter the period of salam the higher the price and the greater the profit. However, it is pertinent to **differentiate these two special forms of sales transactions; the *Istina'a* and *salam*;**

i. Full payment is required in *salam* whereas it is not necessary in *istisna'a*

ii. The time of delivery is an essential part of sale in *salam* while it is not necessary in *istina'a*.

iii. In *salam*, once the contract is effected it cannot be cancelled unilaterally while the case of *istina'a* can be cancelled before the manufacturer commence job.

iv. The subject of *istisna'a* must be a thing that needs manufacturing while *salam* can be effected on anything whether it needs manufacturing or not

7.1.8 Bai' Al 'Inah (Sale And Buy-Back Agreement)

Bai' al inah is a financing facility with the underlying buy and sell transactions between the financier and the customer. The financier buys an asset from the customer on spot basis. The price paid by the financier constitutes the disbursement under the facility. Subsequently the asset is sold to the customer on a deferred-payment basis and the price is payable in installments. The second sale serves to create the obligation on the part of the customer under the facility.

7.1.9 *Bai' Bithaman Ajil* (Deferred Payment Sale)

This concept refers to the sale of goods on a deferred payment basis at a price, which includes a profit margin agreed to by both parties. Technically, this financing facility is based on activities of buying and selling.[119] Like *Bai' al 'inah*, this concept is also used under an Islamic financing facility. Interest payment can be avoided as the customer is paying the sale price which is not the same as interest charged on a loan.

7.1.10 Bai' Muajjal (Credit Sale)

Literally *bai' muajjal* means a credit sale. Technically, it is a financing technique adopted by Islamic banks that takes the form of Murabahah muajjal. It is a contract in which the bank earns a profit margin on the purchase price and allows the buyer to pay the price of the commodity at a future date in a lump sum or in installments[120]. It has to expressly mention cost of the commodity and the margin of profit is mutually agreed. The price fixed for the commodity in such a transaction can be the same as the spot price or higher or lower than the spot price.

Conclusively, this products discussed is not exhaustive of the products that exist in Islamic banks as they are other conventional loan products that have been converted to be shariah complaint amongst different Islamic banks and new ones have been introduced depending on the approval of the bank's SAC

[119] www.islamic-banking.com/glossary_B.aspx. Retrieved on 31/03/2017. 08:09am
[120] www.islamic-banking.com/glossary_B.aspx. Retrieved on 31/03/2017. 08:09am

Chapter Eight: Islamic Bank Security (Collateral)

8.1 Concept of Security

Security (Collateral) in Shariah is called *Ar-rahn.* The term "*rahn*" is commonly used in *fiqh al-muamalah.* According to Shariah (Islamic law), the definition of *rahn* is: "To make an object with economic values in Islamic law perspective as a trust for the payment of debts, so that enabling mortgagee (*Murtahin*) to get all or a part of the debts from the object"[121]

Ar rahn refers to a "possession offered as a security for a debt so that the debt will be taken from it in case the debtor failed to pay back the due money"[122] Imam Abu Zakaria al- Anshary defines *rahn* as "To make an economic object as a trust for the payment of debts, from which unsettled debts are paid[123]". *Ar rahn* has been classified into two (2)[124]

i. **Possessory Rahn:** - A *rahn* is said to be possessory if there is a transfer of possession in the subject matter of the security from the debtor (*al rahin*) to the creditor (*Al Murtahin*). For example, where a pledge or pawn is taken as security.

ii. **Non- Possessory Rahn:** - A *rahn* is said to be non-possessory whereby the title in the subject matter of the security is passed from the debtor to the creditor. As in the case of a mortgage where the title in the landed property is passed to the mortgagee by the mortgagor. Thus it can be seen as a proprietary *rahn.*

However, within Quranic exegesis Ibn Kathir is one of the scholars that explained very well about *Ar rahn* regarding surah al Baqarah verse 283 (al Qurashi, 1999). Bukhari and Muslim alone have recorded at least ten to eleven text of various degree of hadiths about ar-rahn in their respective books[125]. Other great names such as Ibn Abidin, al Shaybani, al-Ḥaṣkafi and al- Shaybaniarakhsi of Ḥanafi, al-Mawardi, al-Syirazi, al-Rafiʿi and al-Nawawi of Shafi'i, al-Dasuqi, al- Dardir, al-Khalil and al-Qarafi of Maliki as well as Ibn Qudamah of Ḥanbali are indeed become "a

[121] Maudila R. L "The optimizing of Rahn service for the Development of Islamic Banking in Indonesia". *Journal of Islamic Economics.* Vol 4, No.2. (2003): Pp.170-171

[122] Nasar S and Khan A.J ," Collateral (Ar-Rahn) as practiced by Muslim funds of North India". J-KAU*: Islamic Economics.* Vol 17, No. 1(2004): Pp.17-34

[123] Abi Zakariya al-Anshari, *Fath al-Wahab* (Singapura: Sulaiman Mariy, n.d.), pp. 192.

[124] Abd.Rahman A. Z, "Collateral and Security in the Islamic Commercial Law: The Concept and operation of Rahn. *Applied* Shariah-Lecture 4. (2009): P. 4

[125] Ṣaḥiḥ Bukhari (al-Bukhari, 810-870M/194 – 256H) no. 2068, 2200, 2252, 2386, 2509, 2511, 2512, 2513 and Ṣaḥiḥ Muslim (al-Nisaburi) (1015-1016M). No: 1603/124-126, p.1226 and 1919

living legend" to the modern scholars in Islamic law. Their great collections on ar-rahn issues had flourished through their meticulous process and methodology developed by them[126].

8.2 Position of Security or Collateral (Ar Rahn) in Islamic Banking

The position of *Ar rahn* secured its support from the Quran and the Sunnah. The Holy Quran states that;

"Every person is a pledge for what he has earned (Deed)"[127].

In shariah law, it means holding something that has a value while giving something on debt. The Quran has laid down this condition in Quran 2: 283 which states that

" And if you are on a journey and cannot find a scribe, then let there be a pledge taken (Mortgaging); then if one of you entrust the other, let the one who is entrusted discharge his trust (faithfully), and let him be afraid of Allah, his lord. And conceal not the evidence for he, who hides it, surely his heart is sinful. And Allah is All-knower of what you do"

The Prophet (SAW) says as narrated by Aisha that;

"The prophet (SAW) purchased food grain from a jew on credit and mortgage his iron armour to him". [128]

In a related hadith from Anas that;

"The prophet mortgaged his armour to a jew in Madinah and bought barley bread from the jew for his family"[129]

From the above narrations presented from the Holy –Quran and the Sunnah, it is explicitly clear that *Ar-rahn* is highly permissible in Shariah thus necessitate the need for its adoption by Islamic banks in doing the business of

[126] Shariff, D, Shaharuddin, A, Muhamed, A.N, Pauzi, N. S, Mohammed, Z. M , " The improvement of Ar-Rahn (Islamic Pawn Broking) Enhanced Product in Islamic Banking System" *Asian Social Science*. Vol. 9, No.2. (2013):Pp 36-37

[127] Quran 2: 283

[128] Bukhari, 48:4

[129] Sahih Bukhari No. 1927, *Kitab al-Buyu-* Ahmad, Nasai and ibn Majah. In Maudila R. L "The optimizing of Rahn service for the Development of Islamic Banking in Indonesia". *Journal of Islamic Economics*. Vol 4, No.2. 2003:Pp.170-171

lending. *Ar rahn* is built upon certain pillars and conditions which majority of the Islamic jurist has agreed upon[130]. These are:-

1. Offer and acceptance (*sighah*)

2. Parties in the *rahn* contract (*rahin* and *murtahin* – the person who provides the collateral and the person who receives the collateral)

3. Collateral asset (*marhun*)

4. The debt itself (*marhun bih*)

In addition, for such a pledge to be valid, there exist other conditions which guide its operations[131]

i. Both the mortgagor and the Mortgagee must have the legal capacity (*Ahliyyah*) to possess and dispose of the property. Thus, the mortgage of an insane person or a minor is not valid.

ii. The agreement terms and conditions must be expressed in writing as supported by Quran 2:282 which states that

"When you deal with each other in transactions involving future obligations in a fixed period of time, reduce them into writing....get two witnesses, out of your own two men... ... ..."

iii. The debt as well as the mortgaged property should not be unlawful commodities whose transactions are forbidden under the Shariah.

iv. The indebted party cannot be coerced into putting collateral. Thus, it should be the debtor (rahin) that should enter the rahn contract voluntarily.

v. An orphans property cannot be put up as a collateral by the trustee unless under exceptional circumstances.

vi. The pledge property should be owned by the pledgor otherwise the contract cannot be executed.

---

[130] Saleem, M.Y. *Islamic Commercial Law*. JohnWiley Publisher. Singapore.2012. Pp. 8-94

[131] Doi A . Shariah*: The Islamic Law*. As-Noordeen Press. 7th Edition. Malaysia. 2007. Pp.386-387; Saleem, M.Y. Islamic Commercial Law.. JohnWiley Publisher. Singapore (2012). Pp. 8-94; https://cief.wordpress.com/2006/03/06/contract-of-ar-rahn-defination-and-conditions. Retrieved 26/12/2015. 9:06am

vii. The pledge property should be in existence at the time that the contract of pledge is concluded and it should be capable of being delivered because the creditor must take its possession.

viii. The property held as collateral must be liquid. In other words, the property can be easily converted to cash.

ix. A property conjoined with another property cannot be pledged separately. For instance a House cannot be pledge without the land because possession of a house is not possible without possession of a land nor can it be sold separately

x. The ownership does not change, thus the owner is responsible for the cost of keeping the property even when it is pledge as collateral. Likewise the owner continues to enjoy any secondary benefit of the property.

xi. If the property held as collateral is lost or damage while in possession of the trustee, without any negligence on his part there is no guarantee by the trustee.

xii. The ownership of the property cannot be transfer until the debt settled or the debtor allows for such transaction.

xiii. If the borrower cannot pay back at the expiry of the term, the judge will order the property pledge as collateral to be sold in the open market even if it is the residence of the borrower.

Ar-rahn is been applied in two different ways under the current practice of Islamic banking which is as follows; an instrument for Financing and a Complementary product. Firstly, *rahn* is considered as an instrument of financing most especially in micro financing and that is why it is been seen as an alternative to the conventional pawnshop. Under this arrangement the loan amount will depend on the value of the *marhun* (pledge asset such as gold, Jewelry etc) may be 70% of the pledged asset will be the loan amount and such pledge asset will be given to the pawn shop or known as "*kedai pajak gadai Islam*" as the marhun which will act as a trustee of the pledged asset during the facility period[132]. A fee will be charge based on daily or monthly calculations for its service safe keep of the pledged item until it is reclaimed and the debt is settled

Secondly, ar-rahn acts as a complementary product that is additional transaction (guarantee/collateral) for other products such as *ba'i al-Murabahah* financing. In this case, Islamic banks can detain debtors' mortgaged objects

[132] Maybank . "The Concept of al-Rahn from the Shariah Perspective…." [pdf]. Available at www.maybank2u.com.my>scoe>articles/ Retrieved 26/12/2015. 09:24am

because of transaction.[133]. For instance under house financing or car financing, the Bank (Creditor) normally financed the purchase of such property to enable the customer pays back over a given period of time. Under such arrangement the financed property becomes the *marhun* (Collateral) which the debtor cannot sell off without the permission of the bank. And in case of default, the bank has the authority to sell the house or car to settle the outstanding amount from the sale and credit debtor of the proceeds from the sale of the property if available.

However, the usage of the above applications is in line with the growth of Islamic financial industry especially in regards of types of *marhun* used for *rahn*. Today, modern asset such as shares, *sukuk* certificates etc are being used as collateral in Islamic financing which is a shift from the previously used assets such as gold, jewely etc

[133] Maudila R. L ."The optimizing of Rahn service for the Development of Islamic Banking in Indonesia". *Journal of Islamic Economics*. Vol 4, No.2. (2003). Pp.170-171

Chapter Nine: Major Types of Acceptable Collateral by Islamic Banks

9.0 Introduction

The securities available to both forms of banking are the same but the differences that exist is its structure. In other words the Islamic banking collateral type must be shariah complaint as any securities (collateral) that is not shariah complaint is not acceptable. Though, the reverse is the case when it comes to the conventional form of banking.

9.1 Land as a security

The Holy Quran says; "*Unto him belongeth whatsoever is in the heavens and whatsoever is in the earth and whatsoever is between them, and what so ever is beneath the sod*" while it also observe that "*it is he who hath made the earth subservient unto you, so walk in the paths thereof and eat of his providence. And unto yhim will be the resurrection*" Thus, land has been given to man to keep in trust, to be used wisely for his own benefit[134].

Land as a security does not only refer to the surface of the land but to all gifts of nature such as rivers, oceans, climate, mountains, fishes, mines forest etc as earlier mentioned. Though, one of the basic things that aid the value of land is the improvements such as building.

Therefore, for Islamic banks to as land as a form of security, such must be shariah compliant. i.e. for instance, improvement on lands that are used for activities that are prohibited such as breweries, casinos, etc cannot be accepted as a form of security against lending as they are also considered as accomplices to the illegal activities.

"*The messenger of Allah cursed the eater of usury and the one who pays usury it, those who witness it and the one who writes it down"* ***(Ibn Majah and Sahih Muslim)***[135]

From the above hadith, we can deduce that all parties involved whether directly or indirectly are cursed by Allah (SWT), so why should we accept improvement that aid illegal activities? However, the reverse is the case when it comes to the conventional banks as they don't consider when the activities used by the improvement are prohibited or not.

---

[134] Shattar, N. "Land Rights in Islam". Dawn news. (2015); Available at www.dawn.com/new/1154522. Retrieved on 02/01/2015. 5:43pm

[135] Ibn Majah, Book 12-Business Transactions, Hadith no. 2363 and Sahih Muslim-Book of Transactions Vol.5, Hadith no. 3380

Furthermore, under the Islamic banking approach when it comes to land as a collateral, mortgage is also created which can either be a legal or equitable mortgage and they also consider other conditions or factors before accepting land as a security apart from the activities such land (improvement) is been used for. Amongst which are borrower's title must be good and registered at the land registry, it must be free from any existing charge or encumbrances, it must be of commercial value etc

9.2 Debenture as a Security

Debenture and it form or types have been discussed in our previous chapters. Though under the Islamic banking approach, a debenture founded upon loan with interest is non-shariah compliant [136]because interest has been prohibited in whatever form under the Shariah law because Allah says. *"O believers fear Allah and give up what is still due to you from interest (Usury), if you are true believers"*. *(Q2:278)* and the prophet (PBUH) has also prohibits *Riba* as reported by Jabir bin Abdullahi "*The messenger of Allah (PBUH) cursed the recipient of usury and its giver, and the one who records it, and the two withness; and he said: "They are all equal (in sin and penalty)"*

In essence Islamic banks does not accept debenture as collateral against lending if it is based on interest whereas the reverse is the case when it comes to the conventional banks. For example, Islamic banks like CIMB Islamic Bank Berhad, Malaysia have adopted debenture as a form of security but it is structure in such as way that the interest element is expunged.

9.3 Shares as a Security

Share certificates of a company can be used or pledge as a security (*Ar rahn*) for bank lending but one fact remains that the business activities of such company must be Shariah compliant. The company must not engage in business activities that involved pork, alcohol, gambling, nightclubs, casinos, pornography etc. Also other financial ratios such as debt to asset, liquid to total asset, receivable to asset are also considered to determine whether or not the company stock are shariah compliant.

Consequently, in as far as the company's stock or activities is not shariah compliant, its shares certificates cannot be accepted by Islamic banks as collateral against lending but the reverse is the case when it comes to the conventional

[136] Abd.Rahman A. Z "Collateral and Security in the Islamic Commercial Law: The Concept and operation of Rahn. *Applied* Shariah-Lecture 4. (2009). P. 4

bank. Though, they (conventional banks) enjoy both sides in as far as the other factors to be considered before accepting shares such as type of share, valuation, margin, type of mortgage etc as earlier discussed are fulfilled. Charges that can also be created by Islamic banks are either equitable mortgage or Legal Mortgage.

9.4 Takaful (Islamic Insurance) as a Security

Takaful is derived from an Arabic word that means joint guarantee, whereby a group of participants agree among themselves to support one another jointly for the losses arising from specified risk. The Quran say "*And help one another in righteousness and piety, but do not help one another in sin and rancor*"(Q5:2). Anas ibn Malik reported that, A man said "*Oh messenger of Allah, should I tie my camel and trust in Allah or should I untie her and trust in Allah" The messenger of Allah (PBUH) said, Tie her and trust in Allah*[137]. With the above necessitate the need for takaful.

The Shariah Advisory Council (SAC), in its 24th meeting dated 24 April 2002, has resolved that the *takaful* business model based on *tabarru`* and *wakalah* is permissible[138] which also consistent with the resolution of OIC Fiqh Academy which recommends the of *tabarru`* concept in developing *takaful* institution[139]. *Takaful* is based on certain principle namely: *Tabarru* (Donation/Contribution) commitment, Ta'awun or mutual assistance, prohibition of *Riba*, ghaar (Uncertainty) and maysir (Gambling or Speculation).

Takaful is classified into two; General and Family takaful. General *takaful* which is a short term policy renewable periodically according to the terms and conditions of the *takaful* contract. Eg. Motor, fire, employer liability, burglary, machine breakdown, health, fire consequential loss, and marine cargo etc) and family *takaful*. Family takaful is a situation whereby people come together to mutually indemnify one another against any disaster that may befall any member of their family such as sudden death or permanent disability. It is usually offered as a long term policy that cover that may span between 10 and 30 years depending on the structure of the product[140].

However, *takaful* is considered as a secondary security against the primary security in Islamic financing as it is used when the latter is faced with losses arising from specified risk. Thus, it is seen as a supporting security. For instance

[137] Tirmidhi, 2517

[138] Central Bank of Malaysia. Shariah *Resolution in Islamic Finance*. Second Edition. (2010): P.63

[139] OIC Fiqh Academy, *Majallah Majma` al-Fiqh al-Islami*, 1985, 2nd Convention, resolution no. 9 (2/9). In Central Bank of Malaysia. Shariah *Resolution in Islamic Finance*. Second Edition. (2010): P.63

[140] Hassan, K.M, Kayed, N. R and Oseni, A. U . *Introduction to Islamic Banking and Finance; Principles and Practice*. Pearson Educational Ltd. England. First edition. 2013: Pp. 216

the HSBC Amnanah introduced the Home owner *takaful* specifically to provide Islamic insurance coverage for its Home Financing-I customers.

9.5 Guarantee as a Security

Guarantee which is called *Kafalah* in Arabic literally means surety, bail, guarantee, responsibility or amenability. *Kafalah* is of two types; *Kafalah bi al-nafs* (Physical) and *kafalah bi al-mal* (Financial). Physical guarantee is also called *Daman Wajh*- guarantee the safe delivery of another for a specific time. Financial guarantee refers to a pledge given to a creditor by the guarantor that the debtor will pay his debt, fine or any other personal liability thereby joining the latter liability to his principal debtor.

Kafalah can be recourse or non recourse guarantee[141]. Contract of Guarantee is permitted in the *shariah* as obtained in Q12:72[142] and Q3:37[143]. Also the Prophet (pbuh) was reported to have gone for the funeral of a man to pray for his soul. He asked those present at the funeral: "did he leave any wealth?, they replied "No." He asked further, "did he die with any debts outstanding?", they replied "yes, he owed two *Dinār*" (in some narrations three *Dinār*). The Prophet (pbuh) was about to leave when he said "then pray on your companion." Abu Qatadah interceded and said: "I guarantee his debt, Oh Messenger of Allah" and the Prophet (pbuh) then pray on his soul[144].

Guarantee is very essential for a flow of commercial dealings as it gives protection to the debtor and assurance and confidence about repayment to the creditor, thus considered as a security. Guarantee can be a personal or Corporate Guarantee.

9.6 Goods as a Security

Goods are acceptable form of security provided that they are not subject to a sale contract and they are *Shariah* compliant. Islamic banks can also uses pledges which are concluded through the offer and acceptance of a contract. Pledges gives the right to possession of goods been pledge until the debt is repaid.

---

[141] Abikan A. I, *Contract of Kafalah (Guarantee):* A veritable product of Islamic Financing. Pp.200-209.

[142] *They said: "We have lost the (golden) bowl of the king and for him who produces it is (the reward of) a camel load; and I will be bound by it.*"The above verse relates the event of Prophet Yusuf and his brothers where the former feigned the loss of the King's measure and stood guarantor for a reward for whoever retrieve it gave validity to the contract under the Islamic law

[143] *So, her Lord (Allah) accepted her with goodly acceptance. He made her grow in a good manner and* ***put her under the care of*** *Zakariyya (Zechariah)*

[144] Sunanu Abu Dawud, hadith No.3343, vol. 3, p. 247

However, only physical goods that can be pledge not intangible goods because of concern over valuation and repossession. In accepting goods are a form of security there are certain features Islamic banks should take into cognizance, the goods must be non-perishable, tradable, ownership rights established and transferable.

9.7 Cash Deposit as a Security

Islamic bank accepts cash as a form of security against loans and advances. Cash in this case could refers to credit balance in an account. It could be a savings, current or fixed deposit account. Under such arrangement, lien will be placed on such account so that the borrower cannot have access to it until full payment of the debt. The lien and set off are often used in this case because the set off empowers the bank to use the cash or deposit to settle the loan in case of default. It can be mandatory or mandatory[145]. Thirty party customers can also pledge such security on behalf of the borrower.

Also, the conventional fixed deposit certificate can be used as a security for Islamic financing based on the ruling of the SAC, in its 9th meeting dated 25 February 1999, has resolved that conventional Fixed Deposit Certificate (excluding the amount of interest or *Riba*) is a right or asset of the customer. Hence, it may be used as security for Islamic financing[146].

9.8 Domiciliation of Payment as a Security

In every facility granted by the Islamic banks there is a risk called credit risk under which possible diversion of funds by the borrower is an example but in order to mitigate against such risk, domiciliation of is normally executed. Domiciliation of payment refers to a tripartite arrangement (Bank, Borrower, third party) whereby the third party (Employer) undertakes to continue to pay the sum due to the borrower directly to the bank until the facility amount is fully redeemed. Individuals and corporate organization that engages in business that require facility in one way or the other do execute such undertaken to domicile their sales or contract proceeds. This type of security is usually considered as a supporting security in financing and it is mostly accepted from employers whose activities are *shariah* compliant.

[145] Abd.Rahman A. Z. "Collateral and Security in the Islamic Commercial Law: The Concept and operation of Rahn. Applied Shariah-Lecture 4. (2009): P. 4

[146] Central Bank of Malaysia . Shariah *Resolution in Islamic Finance*. Second Edition. 2010. P.57

9.9 Negative Pledge as a Security

Negative pledge is an undertaken usually in written that prohibits the borrower from creating any security interest over its assets without the consent of the lender[147]. The SAC, in its 6th meeting dated 26 August 1998, has resolved that "The consent to the second charge given by the first chargee shall not be construed as waiver of his claim towards the asset under the first charge. In addition, consent of the first chargee shall be given in writing to avoid any dispute"[148].

This form of security is considered as a supporting security which is usually acceptable from borrowers with good credit history, payment history and exercise high level of integrity. It is mostly acceptable from blue chips companies.

9.10 Ijarah Agreement as a Security

Ijarah as a concept refers to "rent out something". This means selling the benefit of use or service for a fixed price or wage. *Ijarah* is applicable to two scenerios[149]; employment of services and the use of asset/properties. *Ijarah* as applicable to services is seen as the employment of services of a person for a return (wages/salaries). Here, the employer of such services is called *Musta jir* while the employee is called *Ajir*. Whereas in the case of asset/properties it is refers to as Leasing; the usage of an asset/property for a time period in return for rent. Here the Lessor is called *Mujir* while the Lessee is called *Musta' ajir* and the rent payable is refer to as *Ujrah*. *Ijarah* is also splitted *Ijarah Thumma Al Bai* (Hire Purchase) and *Ijarah-Wal-Iqtina*

Under this arrangement, there exist an *ijarah* agreement which refers to a document stating the terms and conditions of the *ijarah*. It normally contains the Parties involved, amount, duration, mode of repayment, rights of both parties etc. The fact that there exist no any other collateral apart from the property financed, the property lease agreement serves as the collateral to support the borrowing.

[147] John E. I . "Practice of Banking" CIBN *Exam Distance Learning Pack.* PE III.. Accountancy Training and Publication Ltd. Lagos 2011. Pp. 125-147

[148] Central Bank of Malaysia . Shariah *Resolution in Islamic Finance.* Second Edition. 2010. P.56

[149] Usmani T. M *An Introduction to Islamic Finance..* India Adam Publisher and Distributors. New Delhi. 2010. Pp.157, 158

9.11 Sukuk Certificate as a Security

Islamic *Sukuk* refer to as a certificate of investment of same value of shares representing the ownership of tangible asset of the firm[150]. It is equivalent to bonds but since fixed income, interest bearing bonds are not permissible in Islam, it is structured in such a way to comply with the Islamic *shariah*. *Sukuk* is considered as debt securities which are valuable and tradable in the market, thus its certificates have satisfied the required features of acceptable securities in *rahn* for Islamic financing. The ruling of SAC can be used to buttress this fact "The SAC, in its 30th meeting dated 28 October 2002, has resolved that the Islamic debt securities may be charged in a *rahn* contract. The financing receiver is also allowed to identify the respective securities to be charged in the system without physical transfer of the charged securities to the financier[151]. *Sukuks* can be issued under different structures to accommodate the dynamics of different transactions. Some of these structures include: *Salam, Ijarah, Mudaraba, Musharaka, Murabaha.*[152]

In addition, the Syafii scholars allow the security to be taken and used by the chargor as long as consent of the chargee is obtained. The Maliki scholars, on the other hand, allow "*rahn rasmi/hiyazi*" which is the submission of security through official notes in the registry of relevant authority. This may sufficiently represent the actual submission. These views are clearly consistent with the view of contemporary scholars who allow the utilization of debt securities and *sukuk* as securities for *rahn*.

9.12 Assignment of Debt as a Security

Assignment of debt which is called *hiwalah* or *hawalah*. *Hiwalah* is a contract which caused the transfer of debt from one party to another. The participants involved in this contract are the principal debtor, the creditor and the transferee. This contract is permissible as the prophet (SAW) "*The deferment (of paying debt) by the richer is an injustice. When there is one of you, get the offer from one other to transfer your debt to another person, just accept it.*"[153]

---

[150] AAOIFI SS17

[151] Central Bank of Malaysia . Shariah *Resolution in Islamic Finance.* Second Edition. 2010. P.58

[152] Oladunjoye O. M . "Sukuk as a tool for infrastructural development in Nigeria". *Journal of Islamic Banking and Finance*, Vol 2, No1. (2014)." Pp 338-339

[153] http://www.investment-and-finance-net/islamic finance/h/hiwalah.html. Retrieved on 16/12/2015

Hiwalah can be *Hiwalah Muqayyadah* (Restricted Hiwalah) and *Hiwalah Mutlaqah* (Absolute hiwalah)[154]. The borrower can assign debt to the bank as security for credit facility. Under this arrangement the debt in favour of the borrower from the third party is assigned to the bank for the obligation which the former has to the bank. Thus the borrower debtor is expected to settle his debt by paying the bank to which the debt is assigned.

9.13 Letter of Comfort or Awareness

Islamic banks also accept Letter of comfort as security against loan and advances mostly from organizations whose activities are *shariah* compliant. This form of security only creates moral obligation on the part of the issuer rather than a legal obligation which implies that it does not serve as a guarantee to its subsidiary in case of default. Letter of comfort is usually prepared on the issuer letter headed paper duly signed under sealed by two directors or a director and the company secretary.

9.14 Islamic Banks Money Market Instruments as security

Islamic Money Market refers to a market where short term *shariah* compliant funds are raised. By so doing, the market utilizes different types of instruments such are Islamic treasury bills, Islamic Negotiable Instruments, Islamic Commercial Papers etc. These instruments can also be used as collateral against lending considering the fact that they are liquid, tradable and asset backed instruments.

Let briefly discussed, some of the instruments earlier mentioned[155]

i. Islamic Commercial Paper

This is considered as a short term paper issued by corporate at a discount with 1-12months maturities with option of rollover and it is redeemed at par (subject to approval of SAC).

[154] Sahih Bukhari Vol 3.No.487

[155] Federick, R (2014). Islamic Money Market-Islamic Interbank Money Market. Available at:http://islamicfinancialsystem1.blogspot.com.ng/2013/08/Islamic-money-market-islamic-interbank.html; Nur A (2014).Islamic Money Market Instruments. Available at:https://prezi.com/m/onxyg4qq13bd/Islamic-money-market-instrument. Retrieved on 23/04/2017.15:32am; www.rhbgroup..com/products-and-services/business/islamic/islamic-treasury/inslamic-money-market-instruments. Retrieved on 23/04/2017.15:05am

ii. Islamic Treasury Bills

They are issued by the government to meet its short term expenditure. This instrument is structured on the basis of Bai al Inah and has a maturity (ies) period of 3, 6 and 12 months.

iii. Islamic Negotiable Instruments

It is usually structured based on *Mudharabah* or *Bithaman Ajil*. This instrument is made up of two variants; Islamic Negotiable Instruments of Deposit (INID) and Negotiable Islamic Debt Certificate (NIDC). The Islamic Negotiable Instrument of Deposit is similar to the Certificate of Deposit as obtained in the conventional money market. The INID is based on *mudharabah* contract. It involves sum of money deposited with Islamic banks which is repayable at a specified future date at the face value plus dividend.

The NIDC involves the sales of banking institution's asset to the customer at an agreed cash basis and subsequently, the asset is purchased back from the customer at principal value plus profit and to be settled at an agreed future date. This is usually based on the *bithaman Ajil* contract.

Chapter Ten: Islamic Banking Vs Conventional Banking

10.1 Introduction

There are marked differences between the conventional banking and the Islamic banking system. These differences can be seen as a similitude of the difference between the plant cell and animal cell in modern biology. However, one of the major difference between the Islamic banking and the conventional bank is anchored on the fact that Islamic banking is built on *Shariah law*; that's all its products, investment, business focus/approach, lending are in conjunction with the *sharia law*. For easy understanding, it is paramount to split the differences based on the following heading which was culled from the works of Abunme and Alo (2009):-

10.2 Differences between Islamic Banking and Conventional Banking

10.2.1 Differences Prohibition of Interest

Islamic banks neither charge nor pay interest on loans. These prohibitions of interest on loan transactions got its divine support from the holy books (Holy Quran and Bible) as earlier sited. But rather it replaced the interest elements with the profit and Loss sharing structure. In other words, their lending is principally of the Murabahah cost-plus or mark-up mode. Whereas the conventional banking system permits interest in all its loan transactions which is a man-made idea and with string conditions attached to such loan.

10.2.2 Based on Ethics of Islamic *Shariah*

Islamic banks operate in accordance with the rules of *Shariah* known as *Fiqh al Muamalat* (Islamic rules on transactions). These rules place more emphasis on morality when it is related to Islam. In lieu of this, Islamic banks are prohibited from investing in businesses that are considered immoral, or *haraam* e.g. businesses that sell alcohol or pork, gambling, and businesses that produce media such as gossip columns or pornography. This is contrary with to the conventional banking because in their bid to make profit at all cost they invest in areas/commodities that are prohibited. For example, financing of Breweries Company that produce alcoholic drinks etc. In essence, there exist no moral or ethics in this system of banking.

10.2.3 Emphasis on Collateral

Islamic banks places less emphasis on collaterals compared to conventional banks as it is concerned with the viability of the project and the profitability of the operations but not the size of the collateral. This is also supported in the words of G.O Nwankwo that *"There should be no such thing as lending against security as the sole or primary criterion.... In the final analysis, when the crunch comes, the asset may have little resale value. Even then, collecting funds through liquidation of pledged security is an unpleasant business"*. But, the conventional banks primarily focused on collateral as criteria for lending despite customer huge account turnover.

However, the differences between these forms of banking can also be seen in the works of Ust. Hj Zaharuddin Hj Abd rahman (2007) which is presented in a tabular form below;

Conventional Banks	Islamic Banks
1. The functions and operating modes of conventional banks are based on fully manmade principles.	1. The functions and operating modes of Islamic banks are based on the principles of Islamic **Shariah.**
2. The investor is assured of a predetermined rate of interest.	2. In contrast, it promotes risk sharing between provider of capital (investor) and the user of funds (entrepreneur).
3. It aims at maximizing profit without any restriction.	3. It also aims at maximizing profit but subject to **Shariah** restrictions.
4. It does not deal with ***Zakat.***	4. In the modern Islamic banking system, it has become one of the service-oriented functions of the Islamic banks to be a ***Zakat*** Collection Centre and they also pay out their ***Zakat.***
5. Lending money and getting it back with compounding interest is the fundamental function of the conventional banks.	5. Participation in partnership business is the fundamental function of the Islamic banks. So we have to understand our customer's business very well.
6. It can charge additional money (penalty and compounded interest) in case of defaulters.	6. The Islamic banks have no provision to charge any extra money from the defaulters. Only small amount of compensation and these proceeds is given to charity. Rebates are give for early settlement at the Bank's discretion.
7. Very often it results in the bank's own interest becoming prominent. It makes no effort to ensure growth with equity.	7. It gives due importance to the public interest. Its ultimate aim is to ensure growth with equity.
8. For interest-based commercial banks, borrowing from the money market is relatively easier.	8. For the Islamic banks, it must be based on a Shariah approved underlying transaction.

9. Since income from the advances is fixed, it gives little importance to developing expertise in project appraisal and evaluations.	9. Since it shares profit and loss, the Islamic banks pay greater attention to developing project appraisal and evaluations.
10. The conventional banks give greater emphasis on credit-worthiness of the clients.	10. The Islamic banks, on the other hand, give greater emphasis on the viability of the projects.
11. The status of a conventional bank, in relation to its clients, is that of creditor and debtors.	11. The status of Islamic bank in relation to its clients is that of partners, investors and trader, buyer and seller.
12. A conventional bank has to guarantee all its deposits.	12. Islamic bank can only guarantee deposits for deposit account, which is based on the principle of ***al-wadiah,*** thus the depositors are guaranteed repayment of their funds, however if the account is based on the *mudarabah* concept, client have to share in a loss position..

Source: Ust Hj Zaharuddin, A (2007): Differences between Islamic and conventional banks,Senarai Lengkap Artikel, http://zaharuddin.net/index.php?option=com. Retrieved on Tuesday, 29 November 2016. 15:38

10.3 Similarities between Islamic and Conventional Banks

10.3.1 Profit Motive

Both forms of banking are in business to make profits and not losses but the way and manner the profits are made marks a difference. This motive has impact on their investment decisions because their funds are channel into sectors/area with high returns.

10.3.2 Nature of Banking Services

Islamic banks offer the same set of banking services provided by conventional banks, although the operational modes differ in some areas. Islamic banks offer the broad range of payment facilities – clearing mechanisms, bank drafts, bills of exchange, travelers' cheques, etc. –that conventional banks provide. They also offer the three conventional categories of deposit accounts, viz: current accounts, savings accounts, and investment accounts. Like conventional banks, cheque books are issued to holders of current accounts in Islamic banks.

Conclusion

Conventional banking system has been in existence for so many decades now and one notable features that is been attributed to it is that it is interest based. Due to its long existence, it has well established itself in almost all the nooks and cronies of every economies of the world. Consequently this has given it an edge over other form of banking system because they virtually have all the required frameworks and products that will ensure its smooth operations. Islamic banking is still a growing industry and despite its emergence to the financial landscape in the early 70's it has succeeded in competing tremendously with other financial institutions

Islamic banks are also profit seeking institution just like the conventional banks but its modus operandi differs as it operates within the ambit of the shariah law. For it to work perfectly it is guided with certain principles amongst which are prohibition of interest, Gambling and Speculation (Maysir), Gharar, investment in prohibited commodities such as alcohol, pork etc and also it is based on profit and loss Sharing etc

Both the conventional and Islamic system of banking are considered as financial intermediaries as they both have the core mandate to mobilize funds from surplus areas to deficit areas but their approaches differs. However, the conventional bank have a large bouquet of products that aid deposit mobilization which is interest based but the Islamic banking system also leverages on the existing conventional products to modify it so as to be shariah compliant and also introduces new products.

Therefore, the said funds cannot remain idle in the banks as it has to be invested so as to make profit, this also necessitate the need for various credit products to satisfy various needs and taking into cognizance that the said funds needs to be protected by the banks creates the need for collateral. Taking collateral (Ar-rahn) against loans and advances by Islamic banks is highly permitted by the Shariah because the Quran, Hadith and as well as the fatawah amongst Muslim jurist permits the use of collateral to secure a loan so also to the conventional banks.

The application of ar rahn in the business of lending is to as safeguard the interest of the creditors (Islamic banks) majorly with regards to minimization of associated risks and by ensuring that the customers fulfils the duties of a debtor in the most efficient and secure manner. Under the current banking practice, the way and manner which ar rahn is applied as earlier mentioned will enhanced the economy thus ensuring that the core objectives of Islamic economies is achieved, but one issue of concern is that should it be a primary criteria against lending?

Though, under the Islamic banking system they concentrate on the viability and profitability of the project or business to be financed and not the size of the collateral which is a clear deviation from the conventional banking system. This is further supported in the words of a non-muslim scholar Nwankwo (1991) that "There should be no such thing as lending against security as the sole or primary criterion.... In the final analysis, when the crunch comes, the asset may have little resale value. Even then, collecting funds through liquidation of pledged security is an unpleasant business".156

However, collateral arrangement is bedeviled with the issue of realization upon default by borrowers because of constraints such unresolved fiqh issues, the existing legal framework guiding its processes, delayance in the administration of justice, lack of financial court etc all this has made Islamic banks and as well as the conventional bank toothless bull dog in realizing its Non Performing Loan (NPLs) that are secured with collaterals.

[156] Nwankwo, G.O . *Bank Management: Principles and practice*, Malthouse Press Limited. Lagos. 1991:P. 130. In Onyiriuba L . *Analysing and Managing Risk of Bank Lending*. NFS Data Bureau Ltd. Lagos. Second Edition. 2008. Pp. 373

AUTHOR'S BIOLGRAPHY

Ibrahim Mohammed Lawal is bank staff at Heritage Bank Maiduguri, Borno State currently heading the Credit and Marketing Unit. Ibrahim received his BSc in Economics, PGD Mgt from University of Maiduguri and MSc in Economics from the same University.

Ibrahim is a Chartered Banker and a Professional Manager with certification from the Chartered Institute of Bankers of Nigeria (CIBN) and Nigeria Institute of Management (NIM). He is a an Associate Member of the Chartered Institute of Securities & Investment (ACSI-UK), Chartered institute of Islamic Finance Professionals (CIFP-Malaysia), member of Nigeria Economics Society (NES), Institute of Islamic Banking and Insurance (IIBI-UK), Student Member, Association of Certified Chartered Economist (ACCE) and a student member, Chartered Institute of Stock Brokers (CIS), Nigeria.

With over 10years of Banking experience and commitment earned him the award-Branch Most Customer Centric staff and commendation letters from the Managing Director (MD/CEO). Ibrahim has attended numerous trainings and has published the following papers in different journals. He is currently married with two (2) lovely children.

www.ingramcontent.com/pod-product-compliance
Lightning Source LLC
LaVergne TN
LVHW082352200926
848481LV00012B/3543
* 9 7 8 1 6 2 2 6 5 1 5 5 9 *